LOUIS CLARK VANUXEM FOUNDATION

NATURE'S SIMPLE PLAN

A PHASE OF RADICAL THOUGHT IN THE
MID-EIGHTEENTH CENTURY

BY

CHAUNCEY BREWSTER TINKER

PROFESSOR OF ENGLISH LITERATURE IN
YALE UNIVERSITY

PRINCETON
PRINCETON UNIVERSITY PRESS

LONDON: HUMPHREY MILFORD
OXFORD UNIVERSITY PRESS

1922

𝕻𝖗𝖎𝖓𝖈𝖊𝖙𝖔𝖓 𝖀𝖓𝖎𝖛𝖊𝖗𝖘𝖎𝖙𝖞

THE LOUIS CLARK VANUXEM FOUNDATION
LECTURES FOR 1922

THE LOUIS CLARK VANUXEM FOUNDATION
OF PRINCETON UNIVERSITY

was established in 1912 with a bequest of $25,000 under the will of Louis Clark Vanuxem, of the Class of 1879. By direction of the executors of Mr. Vanuxem's estate, the income of the Foundation is to be used for a series of public lectures delivered in Princeton annually, at least one half of which shall be on subjects of current scientific interest. The lectures are to be published and distributed among schools and libraries generally.

The following lectures have been published:

The Theory of Permutable Functions, by Vito Volterra.

Lectures delivered in Princeton in connection with the dedication of the Graduate College of Princeton University, by Emile Boutroux, Alois Riehl, A. D. Godley, and Arthur Shipley.

Romance, by Sir Walter Raleigh.

A Critique of the Theory of Evolution, by Thomas Hunt Morgan.

Platonism, by Paul Elmer More.

Human Efficiency and Levels of Intelligence, by Henry Herbert Goddard.

Philosophy and Civilization in the Middle Ages, by Maurice De Wulf.

The Defective Delinquent and Insane, by Henry A. Cotton.

OMAI, THE SOUTH SEA ISLANDER.
From an engraving by John Jacobs, after a portrait by Sir Joshua Reynolds.

PREFATORY NOTE

In this study of the theory of simplicity—the way of Nature—in the England of 1770, I have begun with an essay intended to set forth the general conviction that civilisation had somehow or other failed of its goal—was at least on the decline—and that primitive man, in his savage or even animal state, was better off than the citizens of Europe. The dream of a finer nation, conceived in simplicity and liberty, in which the arts, and particularly poetry, might flourish as in their native soil, is the subject of the paper on Corsica which forms the second essay.

But simplicity is not of the future only. There must have been a time, far back in the childhood of the nation, when untutored genius sang forth its passion unrestrained by the doctrines of the schools and the narrowing influence of caste; perhaps even now such bards may be found in some remote island. The third essay is therefore entitled *Ancient Bard and Gentle Savage.* Perhaps, untrained by schools and free from the trammels of a conscious art, which is ever growing more artificial, native genius may even now be seeking expression in poetry rude but wildly

v

sweet.   This is the subject of the last essay on the *Inspired Peasant*.

The phrase, 'Nature's simple plan,' is from an anonymous poem on Otaheite, published in 1774, a phrase which was evidently part of the literary jargon of the day.   As late as Wordsworth we find 'Nature's holy plan' (*Lines written in Early Spring*) and 'simple plan' (*Rob Roy*).   Numerous eighteenth century parallels might be cited.

My choice of such a theme at this particular moment hardly requires comment.

C.B.T.

London, January 11, 1922.

NATURE'S SIMPLE PLAN

I

THE STATE OF NATURE

The difference between the savage and civilised state of man has been much considered of late years, since so many discoveries of distant regions and new nations have been made under his present majesty's patronage, and since an eloquent writer upon the continent and even a learned judge who is an author in our own island have thought fit to maintain the superiority of the former.

—Boswell, HYPOCHONDRIACK.

In the spring of the year 1773, four of the most distinguished gentlemen of their day, who had met together at dinner, were engaged in discussing a topic of current and vital interest. The four men were General Oglethorpe (the host), Dr. Samuel Johnson, James Boswell and Oliver Goldsmith; and the theme of their conversation was the menace of luxury. On this perennially engaging topic each of the four men had the clearest convictions, but neither on this occasion nor in subsequent discussions did they discover a common ground of agreement. Had it looked, at any moment, as though they might attain to an easy or courteous unanimity of opinion, Boswell would probably have thwarted them; for unanimity puts an end to discussion, and it was Boswell's office to keep the talk going. Johnson, of course, would listen to no denunciation of the age in which he lived; but Goldsmith had no such loyalty. He expatiated on the degeneracy of the nation, and assigned as the cause of the general decline the insidious vice of luxury. To this Johnson at once demurred, contending that not only were there as many tall men in England as ever—proof that the national stature was not on the decline—but also, since luxury could reach but few persons, it was no real menace. 'Luxury,' he said, 'so far as it reaches the poor, will do good to the race of the people: it will strengthen and multiply them. Sir, no nation was ever hurt by luxury.'

The words of General Oglethorpe on this occasion are not recorded, but in a subsequent conversation he remarked, as an old soldier might have been expected to do, that, inasmuch as what we call the best in life depends upon our own attitude of mind, it is obviously wrong to overestimate the physical comforts of civilisation. Thereupon he quoted Addison's description of the Numidian savage, in *Cato*:

> Coarse are his meals, the fortune of the chase,
> Amid the running stream he slakes his thirst,
> Toils all the day, and at the approach of night,
> On the first friendly bank he throws him down,
> Or rests his head upon a rock till morn;
> And if the following day he chance to find
> A new repast or an untasted spring,
> Blesses his stars, and thinks it's luxury.[1]

On this occasion, however, it was Goldsmith who denounced modern luxury and the 'degenerate times of shame' in which he lived. This had, in truth, become his characteristic vein, though perhaps not his genuine conviction. Three years before, he had published *The Deserted Village,* in which, to use his own words, he 'inveighed against luxury,' and in which he had proceeded to the melancholy conclusion that the rural virtues were deserting England. Piety, Loyalty and faithful Love—to make use of those allegorical capitals which the age affected—were departing with the emigrants to America; and along with them— also to America—was going the Muse of Poetry, to whom, at the end, the author addresses an eloquent though mournful farewell. In the new

---

[1] The lines are quoted as given in the *Life of Johnson* (Hill's ed.), vol. 3, p. 282.

world, the Muse, if she try her voice, is admonished to teach erring man a lesson (of the need of which the poet seems to have had a prophetic realisation)—to spurn 'the rage of gain.'

> Teach him that states of native strength possest
> Though very poor, may still be very blest.

Perhaps, as I have intimated, Goldsmith was less concerned about this vice of luxury than he himself was aware, for, as a matter of fact, he cared not at all for the primitive blessings of rocky pillow and untasted spring so dear to Cato and Oglethorpe. He loved the good things of civilisation quite as well as did his friend Johnson, and, in truth, sometimes snatched at those beyond his reach. Nevertheless he was presumably sincere in his view that poetry flourishes only in a civilisation much simpler than any which he had known. Men like Johnson and Goldsmith might, one would suppose, dismiss the decline of civilisation from their fears if it concerned nothing more alarming than a reduction in the number of tall men or an increase in the consumption of tea and spirits; but it was a vital problem indeed if the production of poetry and the arts was to be hindered by the national love of luxury. *Was* poetry declining? Had it become artificial and false? Did it flourish better in 'a state of nature'? These were the really important aspects of the question. Could it be that the arts are not subject to human control, but spring up naturally in a youthful civilisation? If so, we are forced back once more to the original question, Is civilisation so far corrupted that art no longer springs naturally into life?

To these questions no simple reply could be given. To follow nature is obviously desirable. A 'return to Nature,' if peradventure we have got away from nature, is also desirable; but what *is* the state of nature, and how, in the name of all that is reasonable, are we to return to it? There's the rub. But, surely, people may move in the direction of simplicity by renouncing the soft indulgences of civilisation that have proved most perilous? Savages, peasants, animals even, may serve to show us how far we have departed from the norm. To such questions the world of 1770 addressed no slight or casual attention.

Unrivalled opportunities were now offered for a comparison of savage and civilised life. The accession of George III had been marked by a sudden development of the geographical and ethnographical sciences. The single decade of the 'sixties had seen the expeditions of Commodore Byron, Captain Cartwright, James Bruce, Captain Tobias Furneaux, Captain Wallis, and

Lieutenant (later Captain) Cook. In 1764 Byron set sail for the southwest. He brought home stories of a race of splendid giants in Patagonia, who had been seen by the sailors as they were entering the Straits of Magellan. Captain Samuel Wallis rediscovered the South Sea Isles, and named the one which has since been called Otaheite and Tahiti, 'King George III's Island.' Captain George Cartwright, who lived for sixteen years in Labrador, made six voyages out and back during that time, and brought home with him the first Esquimaux who ever visited England. James Bruce penetrated into Abyssinia, and made a valuable study of its primitive culture. To this series of brilliant explorations the voyages of Captain Cook, which began in 1768, formed the splendid climax.

Along with the interest in these voyages there grew up the desire to see and study man in his primitive state. It was recalled that Peter the Wild Boy (known to Swift and Arbuthnot) who had been caught in the woods near Hanover a generation earlier, was still living in England. He was sought out and catechised respecting the state of nature; but, as he had never learned to articulate a score of words, not much of value was discovered. There was a Savage Girl, too, who had been found years before in the woods of

Champagne, and who was still living in France. She went by the name of Mlle. Le Blanc; but this sobriquet, though elegant, was a little inappropriate, for the account of her relates that when she was caught, at the age of nine, she 'seemed black; but it soon appeared after washing her several times, that she was naturally white, as she still continues.' The girl was generally thought to be an Esquimau, who, having been sold into slavery, escaped from her captors or was abandoned by them, and ran wild in the woods, until by chance she reached the banks of the Marne, where she was finally caught by some French peasants. She must have sojourned in the wilderness for a long time, probably for several years, since, when she was discovered, she had lost all use of language and could give no rational account of herself. When found, she was living like a wild cat in a tree. The account of her, published by M. de la Condamine, was translated into English under the supervision of the Scottish philosopher, Lord Monboddo, and published, with a preface from his own pen, in the year 1768. It is a readable little book, though it was intended by the editor merely as a document for the investigation of the state of nature. He laments that, when he saw Mlle. Le Blanc in 1765, she was 'in a poor state of health, having lost all her extraordinary bodily faculties [such as incredibly sharp sight, agility in swimming, and speed in running] and retaining nothing of the savage but a certain wildness in her look and a very great stomach'; nevertheless his Lordship says she is proof that 'the philosopher will discover a state of nature very different from what is commonly known by that name.' He himself used her as an example of his new and startling doctrine that mankind has passed through many stages, 'from the mere animal to the savage, and from the savage to the civilised man.'[1a]

But the supreme excitement was caused by the appearance in London of Omai or Omiah, a South Sea Island savage, who had been brought home by Captain Furneaux after Cook's second voyage to the Pacific. Omai was gentle, courteous, likable—almost, as we shall see later, 'genteel,'—and there was a widespread desire to regard his as the true state of nature. The British reception in the South Seas had been, on the whole, remarkably cordial. The Tongan Islands, for example, had been named by Captain Cook the Friendly Islands. Whether they stood more in need of the blessings of civilisation or civilisation more in need of the lessons of the South Seas was a question which could now be

[1a] *An Account of a Savage Girl*, Edinburgh, 1768, p. xviii.

seriously debated. Horace Walpole, who sneered
at everything, despised the 'forty dozen of islands,' picked up the Lord knows where, which so
far as he could see, had nothing of more in-
trinsic interest about them than 'new sorts of
fleas and crickets,' or hogs and red feathers.
However, he opined that, if properly husbanded,
they might produce forty more wars.[2] But his
was a lonely voice from the seat of the scornful.
The British imagination decked the new islands
in the glowing colours of romance. Here was a
land of perpetual summer, where man was nour-
ished without toil by the indulgence of Nature.
Bread grew on trees and a natural milk flowed
from the cocoanut. Under the palm-tree lay the
child of the South Seas, 'as free as Nature first
made man,' who ever and anon burst into
snatches of song as he paid his passionate court
to the dusky mistress at his side. Ah, here was
Paradise enow!

Does the account seem extravagant? Listen

[2] *Letters*, August 23, 1772; December 2, 1784. The conception
of Tahitan as superior to European civilisation is as old as the
discovery of the island, and the vitality of the notion is shown
by the ever-increasing literature of the South Seas. Of the influence of Tahiti on the character of Torquil and his companions,
Byron says in *The Island* (2.268) that it

> Tamed each rude wanderer to the sympathies
> Of those who were more happy if less wise,
> Did more than Europe's discipline had done,
> And civilised Civilisation's son.

to the voice of the poet who in 1774 put forth
anonymously, a poem entitled *Otaheite*:

But Fancy leads us o'er yon Isle to rove,
The Cyprus of the South, the Land of Love.
Here ceaseless the returning seasons wear
Spring's verdant robes and smile through-
　　out the year.
Refreshing zephyrs cool the noontide ray,
And plantane groves impervious shades dis-
　　play.
The gen'rous soil exacts no tiller's aid
To turn the Glebe and watch the infant blade.
Nature their vegetable bread supplies,
And high in air luxurious harvests rise.
No annual toil the foodful plants demand,
But unrenewed to rising ages stand;
From sire to son the long succession trace,
And lavish forth their gifts from race to race.
Beneath their shades the gentle tribes repose;
Each bending branch their frugal Feast
　　bestows.
For them the Cocoa yields its milky flood[3]
To slake their thirst, and feed their temp'rate
　　blood.
No ruddy nectar their pure bev'rage stains,
Foams in their bowl, and swells their kind-
　　ling veins.

　　Their ev'ning hours successive sports pro-
　　　　long,
The wanton dance, the love-inspiring song.

[3] *Cf.* Byron, *The Island*, 2.256 ff.

Impetuous wishes no concealment know,
As the heart prompts the melting members
   flow.
Each Oberea[4] feels the lawless flame
Nor checks desires she does not blush to
   name.

No boding presage haunts them through
   the night,
No cares revive with early dawn of light.
Each happy day glides thoughless as the last,
Unknown the future, unrecalled the past.
Should momentary clouds, with envious
   shade,
Blot the gay scene and bid its colours fade,
As the next hour a gleam of joy supplies,
Swift o'er their minds the passing sunshine
   flies.
No more the tear of transient sorrow flows,
Ceased are the lover's pangs, the orphan's
   woes.[5]

All this is not merely a poet's dream. Many
took such statements literally. Lord Monboddo,
in a serious scientific work, asserted in so many
words, that the Golden Age yet lingered in the
islands of the South Seas,[6] 'where the inhabitants

4 Oberea was queen of Otaheite.

5 From *Otaheite*, London, 1774, an anonymous poem. My friend,
Professor Collins of Princeton calls my attention to the fact that
a selection from this poem appeared in the *Pennsylvania Magazine* for March, 1775.

6 *Origin and Progress of Language*, Second ed., 1774; 1.226n.,
390 n.

live without toil or labour upon the bounty of
Nature.' In Otaheite, he says, 'the inhabitants
pull bread off trees, which grow with no culture,
for about nine months of the year, and when this
food fails, it is supplied by nuts and other wild
fruits.'

Boswell, who knew Captain Cook, expressed a
wish to go and live for three years in Otaheite, in
order to meet with people so different from any
that had yet been known, 'and be satisfied what
nature can do for man.' [7]

We have reached this point without mention
of Rousseau. It would, perhaps, be possible to
avoid it altogether, for, in truth, Rousseau was
not at this time widely read or generally popular
in England. Important as was his later influence, it was slight in comparison with the im-
press made upon the national mind by Captain
Cook in the decade of the 'seventies. Nevertheless, Great Britain had her student and critic
of Rousseau. James Burnet, more generally
known by his judicial title, Lord Monboddo, may
be called the Scottish Rousseau,[8] for he held the

[7] *Life of Johnson,* ed. Hill, vol. 3, p. 59.

[8] Among other references to Rousseau, see his *Origin of Language* 2d ed. 1.403 and 414 *n,* and *Antient Metaphysicks,* 3.233.
Chapter XII in the first volume of the former work is avowedly
an attempt to solve 'Mons. Rousseau's great difficulty with respect
to the invention of language.' In the preface to the *History of*

savage mode of existence superior to civilised life.
It was he who first applied to the study of the
'state of nature' the historical or evolutionary
method as opposed to the older philosophic or
'systematic' method. Monboddo's chief claim to
remembrance—a recognition which science has
not even grudgingly accorded him—is his doctrine of a gradual progression of living things
from a rudimentary to a more developed state.
In his study of this progression he anticipated
some important conclusions of the nineteenth
century: 'In all natural things,' he wrote, 'there
is a progress from an imperfect state to that
state of perfection for which, by nature, the thing
is intended. This is so evident to me that, from
theory only, though it could not be proved by
facts, I should believe that man was a mere animal before he was an intelligent being, and that
there was a progression in the species such as we
are sure there is in the individual.'⁹

The man who wrote those words might, I
should suppose, fairly be reckoned among the

the *Wild Girl* Monboddo says that Rousseau is the 'only philosopher of our time' who has conceived the *magnum opus* of philosophy to be 'to inquire whether, by the improvement of our faculties, we have mended our condition and become happier as well
as wiser.' But, he adds, though Rousseau had the idea, none has
executed it.

⁹ *Antient Metaphysics,* vol. 3, p. 282.

forerunners of Herbert Spencer; but when he is referred to at all, Monboddo is called a predecessor of Darwin. This is because he contended that the orang-outang was man in his primitive state. This in itself was sufficient to draw upon him the ridicule of his contemporaries; for though they were eager to assert the essential nobility of the savage, they had no disposition to extend their admiration to the animal kingdom and dwell on the simple dignity of orang-outangs. Yet Monboddo, it would seem, might have expected to receive recognition from a later generation to whose habit of thought his own was more naturally related. Two of his contemporaries, it is true, interested themselves in his theories if they did not actually accept them—Robertson the historian and Sir Joseph Banks the botanist, who sailed in Cook's first expedition, and had seen man in his natural state.

But Monboddo had certain faults which exposed him to the derision of his readers, and, indeed, impaired the entire value of his books. He had, for one thing, the credulity of a child, with respect to anything which he wished to believe. Since he had no real acquaintance with primitive man, save what visits to Peter the Wild Boy and Mlle. Le Blanc had given him, this was a ruinous defect. Much of the evidence which he seriously presents for the study of historians and scientists would have disgraced a book written two hundred years before, and some of the more amusing anecdotes would adorn the lighter pages of *Gulliver's Travels*. Monboddo must have been deliberately gulled by practical jokers, returned travellers, and yarn-spinning sailors. He believed nearly everything he was told and all that he found in print. He quoted from Cardinal Polignac the account of an animal in the Ukraine called the *baubacis,* which inhabits caverns underground, makes wars, takes other animals into slavery, and lays up provisions for itself:

They make those slaves lie down upon their back, and hold up their legs, and then they pack the hay upon them, which their legs keep together, and having thus loaded these *living carts,* as our author calls them, they drag them along by the tail. I think it can hardly be doubted that this animal, with so much sagacity, if it had likewise the organs of speech would in process of time, invent a language.[10]

But the most famous of his heresies was his belief in the existence of men with tails. His other lapses from common sense might have been forgotten in time, but his perpetual emphasis on the caudal appendage put all his readers in hysterics:

[10] *Origin of Language,* 1.423.

I could produce legal evidence by witnesses yet living of a man in Inverness, one Barber, a teacher of mathematics, who had a tail about half a foot long which he carefully concealed during his life; but was discovered after his death, which happened about twenty years ago.[11]

In Monboddo's theory the existence of a tail was all-important because it would demonstrate man's relation to the speechless brute.[12] To Monboddo, you see, it was the missing link. Hence his eagerness to discover a man, or, better still, a tribe of men with this useful member. It is related that when James Bruce, the explorer, returned to Scotland from Abyssinia, he went into a court-room where Lord Monboddo was sitting as judge, and that he at once received a note from the noble Lord requesting to be *immediately* informed if he had encountered any men with tails. Such men, he believed,[13] existed in the Dutch East Indies, where they waved their tails like cats—to the edification of an occasional

11 *Origin of Language*, 1.262 *n.*

12 'I have dwelt thus long upon the orang-outang because if I make him out to be a man, I prove by fact as well as by argument, this fundamental proposition, upon which my whole theory hangs, that language is not natural to man. And, secondly, I likewise prove that a natural state of man, such as I suppose it, is not a mere hypothesis, but a state which at present actually exists.' (*Origin of Language*, vol. 1, p. 358.)

13 *Origin of Language*, vol. 1, p. 258.

sailor. What might not Burnet have found in Abyssinia? Contemporaries of Monboddo made merry over this tender pre-occupation of his. An anonymous satirist wrote at some length about the spiritual dangers which might arise from too vain a regard for tails—if we had them:

This rigid Nature, to restrain our pride,
To monkies granted, but to men denyed.[14]

Dr. Johnson, who had met the judge in Scotland as well as in London, said of him: 'Other people have strange notions, but they conceal them. If they have tails, they hide them; but Monboddo is as jealous of his tail as a squirrel.'

There is a famous passage in the *Descent of Man* where Darwin describes one of our presumptive simian ancestors with an eloquence of admiration which scientists usually deny themselves. A somewhat similar enthusiasm was Monboddo's. The satirist quoted above calls him the baboon's 'gen'rous friend,' who 'when brutes can rise no more, makes us descend.' Monboddo convinced himself that orang-outangs live together in society, and frequently act in concert, particularly in attacking elephants, that they build huts to defend themselves against the weather, and 'no doubt practise other arts, both

[14] From *An Heroick Epistle from Omiah to the Queen of Otaheite*, London, 1775. Embryology might have aided Monboddo.

for sustenance and defence.' The animal, he
said, is 'of human form both outside and inside,'
walks upright, makes slaves of men whom he
captures, and (by way of climax) plays the
flute.[15] In disposition he is docile and even af-
fectionate, naturally attached to his master and
to his mate. He is even capable of remorse and
of sensitiveness. Once an orang-outang served as
a sailor on board a Jamaican ship trading to the
Slave Coast. He messed with the crew, and performed the duties of a sailor. He also served
the captain as cabin-boy. One day he had the
misfortune to break a china bowl, and 'the captain,' says our author, 'beat him, which the animal took so much to heart that he abstained from
food, and died.' In short, the orang-outang can
do everything but talk, but even this limitation
of his abilities was not, in Monboddo's eyes, sufficient ground for excluding him from the *genus
homo*. Who can prove that language is natural

[15] See, *Origin of Language,* vol. 1, p. 268, and *Antient Metaphysicks,* vol. 3, pp. 41 ff. Monboddo refused human dignity to
the monkey and even the ape: 'Though I hold the orang-outang
to be of our species, it must not be supposed that I think the
monkey or ape, with or without a tail, participates of our nature.'
(*Origin of Language,* vol. 1, p. 311.)

Goldsmith attacks Monboddo's theory in his *History of Animated Nature* (1774), vol. 4, p. 204, where he says of the orang-
outang: 'All its boasted wisdom was merely of our own making.'
He provides an engraving of the animal, which shows him stick
in hand, with two of his sheds or huts in the middle distance.

to man? Monboddo believed that it was not,
and wrote a treatise on language in three vol-
umes to defend and establish his view.

Monboddo wrangled with Johnson about the
comparative felicity of a savage and a London
shop-keeper, and espoused the cause of the former. Although my acquaintance in both groups
is, unhappily, restricted, I should, if pressed to
a decision, choose as did Monboddo.[16] The
learned judge, you see, preferred the estate which
had the longer and richer future before it. The
London shop-keeper, considered as typical of
modern civilisation, was, he held, facing extinc-
tion. The impoverished life, physical and mental, which he endured in the metropolis, was
but an index of the inevitable disaster which
was to befall him and the social world that had
made him. For Monboddo, unlike some later
evolutionists, dipped into the future, where he
discovered no happy lot for mankind. Civilisation has arrived at the abyss. Modern man—
such as the shop-keeper—is a paltry creature
who, in the general decay, physical and spiritual,
has already reached a stage below that of the
orang-outang. The popularity of such figures as
Mowgli and Tarzan shows that there is a large

16 Johnson confessed to Mrs. Thrale that at another time he
might very probably have argued for the savage.

section of the community—in which, no doubt, are several representatives of the shop-keeping class—who, in sentiment and imagination at least, are not unwilling to revert to a savage state. Monboddo contended that the savage's perfect knowledge of certain facts, such as concern hunting and warfare, more than repays him for his ignorance of general principles.[17] His senses are more acute; he has a variety of exact information derived from instinct, which gives him a foreknowledge of everything necessary to his well-being. He is incredibly stronger than civilised man, and can endure more pain and fatigue. He brings to all his enterprises a patience and perseverance of which modern man is incapable.

As for civilisation, the long story is nearing an end. The decline is now so rapid as to be almost visible, and its stages may be traced from age to age. Warfare alone is enough to make away with us: 'The destruction of modern war is so prodigious by the great armies brought into the field and which are likewise kept up in time of peace, and by the extraordinary waste of men, by fatigue, disease and unwholesome provisions, more than by the sword, while the internal policy of Europe at present is so little

[17] *Antient Metaphysicks*, vol. 2, pp. 157, 313.

fitted to supply such destruction that, unless the
princes either fall upon some other way of de-
ciding their quarrels or provide better for the
multiplication of people, Europe is in the ut-
most hazard of being again depopulated, as it
once was under the Romans, but without the re-
source which it then had of barbarous nations to
repeople it.'[18]   Other causes of decline analysed
by Monboddo[19] were commerce (Goldsmith's
bête noir) and depopulation or emigration (Boswell's) and their result is exhibited in the decreas-
ing stature of man, feebler health, and shorter
life.[20]   In the rapid development of science and
the mechanic arts Monboddo took no comfort,
since he regarded the natural philosophy of his
day as conversant merely with facts and as seldom rising above 'the air-pump and the alembic'.
The science of universals as developed by the
Greeks was the only true source of scientific prin-

18 *Origin of Language,* vol. 1, p. 430.

19 Monboddo's incomplete MSS. contain an outline for an essay
on the *Degeneracy of Man in a State of Society.* See W. Knight,
Lord Monboddo and his Contemporaries, p. 276.

20 This general attitude is also attacked by Goldsmith in his
History of Animated Nature. 'Man,' he says, 'was scarce formed
when he began to deplore an imaginary decay.' He concludes, on
the evidence of antiquities and the fine arts, that men have been
in all ages 'much of the same size that they are at present.' He
admits, however, that our ancestors excel us in the poetic art,
'as they had the first rising of all the striking images of Nature.' To this belief I return in my third essay.

ciples, and its neglect by the new experimental school condemned them to minister to the merely physical needs of man and thus to that softening of fibre which was at once the cause and the symptom of decay.

There is a gusto, a passionate indignation, a satiric force in some of Monboddo's denunciations of the race which point us forward to the style of a later Scot who was also enamoured of invective:

If Momus, quitting his sportive vein, should assume a tone of keen satire and virulent invective, and if M. Rousseau should lend him words, he would say that man is the most mischievous animal that God has made, that he has already almost depopulated the earth, having in many countries destroyed whole specieses [*sic*] of animals, and continuing daily to destroy those that remain, not only to gratify his luxury and vanity, but for mere sport and pastime. 'What attonement [*sic*], most pernicious *biped* or *quadruped* or whatever other title most offends thine ear, what attonement canst thou make for this so great abuse of thy superior faculties and this destruction of the creatures of God? None other except to destroy thyself next, and so avenge the rest of the animal race. This thou art doing as fast as possible, and for this only I commend thee. When this work is accomplished, then shall the true state of nature be restored, and the real

golden age return. Then shall Astraea visit the
earth again, whose latest footsteps are now no
longer to be seen. So shall the rest of the animal creation, freed from a tyrannical and capri-
cious master, live the life which nature has destined for them and accomplish the end of their
being. So shall even man himself, if any of the
wretched race yet remain, acquit providence of
the imputations he has thrown upon it, and shew
that *he was made upright, though he have found
out many inventions.*'[21]

In all the annals of modern nihilism it would
be difficult to cite a destructive mania more extravagant than this; it is, indeed, the climax of
the author's pessimism. Yet in the man himself there was nothing of the Ishmaelite. He was
given to self-discipline. In an age of overeating
his meals were light and frugal. He had a most
undemocratic love of baths, which he took cold,
at the unheard-of hour of six in the morning, and
at a 'bower' near a running stream. He sat
naked in the open air in order to harden himself,
and to protest against the luxury which was lull-
ing the age into effeminacy and decay. He
eschewed all modern 'conveniences.' Even when
going to London he would not make use of a
coach or chaise, but rode all the way on horse-
back.[22] His estates at Monboddo fell into decay,

21 *Origin of Language,* vol. 1, page 414 *n.*
22 In this respect he was but practising the precepts of Rous-

but, as they had been good enough for his ancestors, who were better men than he, he left them unrepaired. He might be condemned by fortune to live in an era of decay, but he could at least rise superior to the self-indulgence all about him.

In commenting on Lord Monboddo's system, Boswell remarked that if savage life were truly desirable, the felicity might be enjoyed by many, since a man might betake himself to the woods whenever he pleased.[23] Boswell had visited Rousseau in his 'wild retreat' in the Val de Travers, where, however, he seems to have found a measure of savage simplicity still lacking. He spoke to Johnson of a man of whom Lord Monboddo knew, who had lived for some time in the wilds of America, and who was wont to reflect: 'Here am I, free and unrestrained, amidst the rude magnificence of nature, with this Indian woman by my side and this gun with which I can procure food when I want it. What more can be desired for human happiness'? Johnson retorted: 'It is sad stuff. It is brutish. If a bull could speak, he might as well exclaim, "Here

seau. The latter philosopher proposed to have no carriages whatever in Corsica. Ladies and priests might ride in two-wheeled chaises; but 'les laïques, de quelques rangs qu'ils soient, ne pourront voyager qu'à pied ou à cheval.' Streckeisen-Moultou, *Oeuvres inédites de Rousseau,* p. 119.

[23] In his *Hypochondriack,* No. 51, *London Magazine.*

am I with this cow and this grass; what being can enjoy greater felicity" '?

The difference between civilised and savage life may be measured either by sojourn among barbaric peoples or by bringing savages into the heart of modern civilisation. In the representatives of a ruder life brought suddenly into the midst of metropolitan life, the world of 1770 displayed an absorbing and a somewhat naïve interest. In the autumn of 1772, Captain Cartwright, the Labrador explorer, brought a family of five Esquimaux on a visit to London. The head of this family was Attuiock, who, in his own country, held the rank of priest; he was accompanied by his youngest wife and her little daughter not yet four years old, his younger brother and the latter's wife, named Caubvick. These people, arrayed in skins and accompanied by an Esquimau dog and a 'beautiful eagle,' caused a convulsion of excitement in the streets of London. Captain Cartwright was so overrun with visitors at his lodgings in Leicester Street that he was obliged to change his residence, and to devote two days a week to exhibiting the Esquimaux. On these days the crowd at his door was so great as to fill up the street in which the house was situated. Among the visitors was James Boswell who went and tried to converse with

Attuiock by signs; this he did by way of testing Monboddo's theory that it was possible to carry on a considerable conversation without spoken words.

The Esquimaux saw King George review some of his troops. The king glanced at the strangers, took off his hat, and smiled. Later they were presented at Court, as well as to 'several of the nobility and people of fashion.' They were taken to the opera and to the play. Colman gave a special performance of *Cymbeline* for them, at which they occupied the royal box. But they lacked the power of response to all these opportunities. Once, after a walk from Westminster Bridge to Hyde Park, Attuiock cried out, 'Oh, I am tired: here are too many houses, too much smoke, too many people. Labrador is very good. Seals are plentiful there. I wish I was back again.'

As the days passed, there was some slight advance in their appreciation of the things about them, but, Cartwright says, no intelligent understanding of their origin or use, any more than 'one of the brute creation' might have. Structures like London Bridge and St. Paul's Cathedral they took for natural objects of gigantic size such as their own ice-cliffs, and even after examination, could hardly believe them to be the work of human hands. In the country—Cartwright removed them to Nottinghamshire in February—they were happier, for there the men took naturally to fox-hunting and the women to dancing. 'The land is all made' was their comment on the English scene.[24]

When Cartwright embarked again for Labrador in May, 1773, the Esquimaux were all well-pleased at the prospect of going home. But the poor creatures had not yet finished with civilisation. On the return voyage they fell ill, apparently with small-pox, and all died except Caubvick, who, bald and emaciated, was restored to her wailing countrywomen. She, more than any other in the little group, had seemed to appreciate the comfort and luxury to which she had been introduced; she is said to have become a graceful dancer. But she resumed her native mode of living with a complacency which occasioned Cartwright, when he saw her again, great surprise.

Omai, the South Sea Islander, who was brought to London in the autumn of the next year, was received with no less enthusiasm than the Esquimaux had been. He, too, was pre-

24 The best account of the Esquimaux in London is found in C. W. Townsend's *Captain Cartwright and his Labrador Journal,* Boston, 1911. See the entry for October 22, 1772, *et seq.*

sented at court; the artists of the day vied with one another in reproducing his features, he became the favourite of Lady Sandwich; and all that the gay and fashionable world could do to pleasure a visitor was done for Omai. He was a much more agreeable person than Attuiock, and showed an appreciation of civilisation that was, superficially, as keen as Attuiock's had been dull. But, when the time came for him to return to his home, the general feeling was that he had gained nothing of lasting worth, and that it would have been better for him if he had been left in his island. The mantle of civilisation slipped easily from the brown shoulders of Omai; but he was never again what he had been before. The touch of the western world, which had not been able to transform him into the image of civilised man, had yet spoiled him for life among his kind.

Those who believed English civilisation to be corrupt found in its effect upon Omai and the Esquimaux plentiful evidence of their contention. Material comforts seemed to them to be shown in their true character as more of a curse than a blessing. But those who took a saner view saw that it was not a question of measuring civilisation by its material possessions, but rather of testing men by their capacity to make a proper use of such 'blessings.' In the last analysis, it is this capacity which distinguishes an Omai from a Pericles, a Caubvick from an Aspasia. I know of no better conclusion regarding the matter than that given by Oliver Goldsmith in a passage now almost forgotten in the *History of the Earth and Animated Nature*.[25] It represents, I think, his reasoned conclusion on this subject of ours, and though it differs radically from the superficial views which he expressed in the conversation quoted at the beginning of this paper, it is none the less characteristic of him—characteristic, moreover, of that finer thought which is always found in his books as distinct from his conversation:

We shall never know whether the things of this world have been made for our use; but we very well know that we have been made to enjoy them. Let us then boldly affirm that the earth and all its wonders are ours; since we are furnished with powers to force them into our service. Man is the lord of all the sublunary creation; the howling savage, the winding serpent, with all the untamable and rebellious offspring of nature are destroyed in the contest or driven at a distance from his habitations. The extensive and tempestuous ocean, instead of limiting or dividing his power, only serves to assist his industry and enlarge the sphere of his enjoyments. Its billows and its monsters, instead of

[25] Ed. 1774; vol. 1, chapter 15.

presenting a scene of terror, only call up the courage of this intrepid little being; and the greatest dangers that man now fears on the deep is [*sic*] from his fellow-creatures. Indeed, when I consider the human race as Nature has formed them, there is but very little of the habitable globe that seems made for them. But when I consider them as accumulating the experience of ages, in commanding the earth, there is nothing so great or so terrible. What a poor, contemptible being is the naked savage, standing on the beach of the ocean and trembling at its tumults! How little capable is he of converting its terrors into benefits or of saying, "Behold an element made wholly for my enjoyment!" He considers it as an angry deity, and pays it the homage of submission. But it is very different when he has exercised his mental powers; when he has learned to find his own superiority and to make it subservient to his commands. It is then that his dignity begins to appear, and that the true Deity is justly praised for having been mindful of man; for having given him the earth for his habitation and the sea for an inheritance.[26]

26 Compare the opening sentences of the book: 'The world may be considered as one vast mansion where man has been admitted to enjoy, to admire, and to be grateful. The first desires of savage nature are merely to gratify the importunities of sensual appetite and to neglect the contemplation of things, barely satisfied with their enjoyment: the beauties of nature and all the wonders of creation have but little charms for a being taken up in obviating the wants of the days, and anxious for precarious subsistence.'

If a man finds civilisation a menace to the
spirit, he would, no doubt, do well to renounce it
and retire into a monastery or even to a lodge in
some vast wilderness. Such retirement is of ob-
vious value, and the regular life is a genuine need
of civilisation in every age. But to renounce the
things of civilisation as well for others as for oneself, or, worse still, for the community at large,
is to make the perilous assertion that there is but
one way to grow in grace. If thine eye offend
thee, pluck it out, but do so with a rational recol-
lection that an eye does not, naturally, cause
offence, and that it may be well for others to keep
their eyes.

The consideration of Nature's simple plan was
carried over into the Romantic Movement, and
may be traced in some of its loveliest manifestations in the work of Wordsworth and of Byron,
of Longfellow and of Thoreau; and the doctrine
of repudiation, limitation, and prohibition, has,
as we are all aware, remained an essential feature
of it. Yet history has, I believe, no outstanding
example of a great civilisation based upon re-
nunciations, except, perhaps, that of Sparta, and
the civilisation of Sparta, when all is said, was
not conspicuous for its art.

II

A NEW NATION

'How end all our victories? In debts and a wretched peace.'

—Horace Walpole.

Since man, by nature, consorts with his kind, Nature's simple plan must be applicable to men in society; there must be, in other words, a 'state of nature' for peoples as well as for individuals. Throughout the century the characteristic marks of such a society were the subject of profound study and brilliant speculation. But where was the model to be found? Some, like Rousseau, despaired of discovering it anywhere in the modern world, could not be certain that such a group had ever existed in the past, and were obliged to admit that the state which was the subject of their inquiries might be merely ideal. Nevertheless it was an ideal possible of attainment and, indeed, as natural and of as much authority in governing the conduct and the political ventures of men as though its existence were actual.

On one characteristic of such a society of men,

all were agreed. It must be free. Of liberty and
the natural rights of man the philosophers of the
seventeenth and eighteenth centuries wrote with
an eloquence that has never been surpassed. It
is not my intention to review their conclusions.
For the purposes of this paper it is sufficient to
say that one of their chief problems was to recon-
cile the existence of personal freedom with that
quantum of authority which is necessary in order
to hold any state together. Concession of some
kind there must be, an equal concession from all
the contracting parties. Equality in the sight of
the law is prerequisite to any such conception of
liberty. Moreover, any notion of equality contains within itself a theory of brotherhood; and
thus the group becomes a family, self-governed,
the members of which owe allegiance to an ab-
straction, a 'state' or 'commonwealth,' whose only
'rights' are those which the component individuals have surrendered to it.

But where was such a model nation to be
found?

'There is,' wrote Rousseau in his *Social Contract,* 'one country still capable of legislation—
the island of Corsica. The courage and con-
stancy with which that brave people have re-
covered and defended their liberty deserves the
reward of having some wise man teach them how

to preserve it. I have a presentiment that this little island will one day astonish Europe."[1] Rousseau was not the only author who had eulogised the Corsicans. King Frederick of Prussia had already written of them a sentence which Rousseau may have known, and in which this 'little handful of brave men' were cited to prove how much courage and natural virtue the love of liberty bestowed upon men.[2]

The words of Rousseau were especially grateful to the Corsicans, insomuch that Buttafuoco, a native Corsican resident on the Continent, wrote to Rousseau in 1761, suggesting to him that he should draw up a plan of government to be used when Corsica should have established her independence. Rousseau, though he did not accept at once, soon made it clear that he would undertake the work. It is difficult to see how he could have declined the offer, once made—the wonder is that it was made at all—for it was a unique opportunity to translate into fact the theory of government stated in the *Social Contract*. But unfortunately Rousseau knew nothing of Corsica; he had never been to the island, and had, at the moment, no desire to go. He shrank from the exertion of such a trip, and complained

[1] Book 2, chapter 10.
[2] *Anti-Machiavel*, chapter 20.

of the amount of baggage which he and the faithful Thérèse would have to carry—linen, books,
kitchen utensils, and even paper on which to
draft the constitution! In order to spare himself, therefore, he wrote to Buttafuoco and demanded all kinds of information, a map, a sketch
of the topography, flora, and fauna of the island,
its history and culture, and an account of the
character of the people. On the basis of what he
learned he began work on the constitution,[3]
which, however, he never completed. It is in
many ways a curiously modern document. Its
references to the *sot orgueil des bourgeois,* its
glorification of manual labour, and its repudiation of money (which is to be tolerated only till
that happy day when it will be worthless), might
have been written yesterday. Liberty, says the
preface or Considération Générale, such as it is
conceived in other European countries, is a
travesty. England, for example, loves liberty
not for itself but only as an opportunity for making money. But what is true liberty? The constitution of Corsica shall answer. On assuming
his rank as a Corsican, every citizen shall swear
the following oath, in the open air, with his hand

[3] See M. G. Streckeisen-Moultou, *Oeuvres inédites de Rousseau,*
Paris, 1861.

upon a copy of the Gospels,[4] and in the presence of his equals:

Je m'unis de corps, de biens, de volonté et de toute ma puissance à la nation corse, pour lui appartenir en toute propriété, moi et tout ce qui dépend de moi. Je jure de vivre et mourir pour elle, d'observer toutes ses lois et d'obéir à ses chefs et magistrats légitimes en tout ce qui sera conforme aux lois. Ainsi Dieu me soit en aide en cette vie, et fasse miséricorde à mon âme. Vivent à jamais la liberté, la justice, et la République des Corses. Amen. Et tous, tenant la main droite élevée, répondront, Amen.

The poverty of Corsica was one of its attractions to Rousseau, for he wished to attach the people to the soil. The sole method of keeping a state independent, he asserted, was by cultivating its soil. He hoped that the population of Corsica might so increase that every fertile inch of the island should be under cultivation. The object was to turn the Corsicans into a nation of farmers, and very literally to beat swords into plough-shares. The island was to be self-supporting and independent of commerce with its neighbours. 'Le seul moyen,' wrote Rousseau, 'de maintenir un Etat dans l'indépendance des

---

[4] The one restriction laid upon Rousseau in his work was that he should not tamper with the Corsican religion. So Paoli told Andrew Burnaby. See the latter's *Journal of a Tour to Corsica.*

autres est l'agriculture.' For this reason his entire plan is a 'système rustique.' Trades and all forms of traffic were to be discouraged, as fit only for the bourgeois with their stupid pride. Indeed the bourgeois 'only disparage and dishearten the laborer.' They congregate naturally in cities, and cities in the *système rustique* are noxious. People are either producers or idlers. As for money and the financial system, they must for a time be tolerated; but presently, if the cultivation of the land is successful, money will become useless. At best it is but a mark and symbol of inequality, and the less it circulates in the island, the more will abundance reign.

Inasmuch as there will be no great fortunes to be made, men will not wish either to desert the farm for the city, or to increase the size of their holdings. Severe penalties were fixed to encourage the people to remain at home. No one was to be allowed to hold land outside his own parish, or *piève;* and any one who moved to another district was to be penalized by the loss of his citizenship. The duty of a Corsican was to stay at home and propagate his kind. With the extirpation of luxury would come health, happiness, tranquillity and large families.

In contrast to this vision of peace and agriculture, we may turn to another account:

Corsica is a vast assemblage of mountains, crowned with primaeval forests and furrowed with deep valleys. At the bottom of these valleys is a little productive soil [*terre végétale*], with a few scattered groups of half savage people, subsisting on chestnuts. These people have not the look of a society of men, but rather seem like a group of hermits, drawn together only by their needs. Thus, though poor, they are not greedy. They think of only two things: taking vengeance on their enemy and courting their mistress. They are replete with a sense of honor, and it must be admitted that it is a more sensible honour than that of 18th century Paris. But on the other hand, their vanity is almost as easily piqued as that of a bourgeois in a village. If, while on a certain road, one of their enemies sounds a cowherd's horn from the top of the neighboring mount, it is no time for hesitation. That man must be killed.[5]

It was estimated that eight hundred Corsicans were lost every year by assassination alone. To Chesterfield, who reflected the view of the diplomats of Europe, the people were a 'parcel of cruel and perfidious rascals'; and even Boswell was shocked by their vendettas. Yet the imagination of the liberals idealised Corsica as a land of 'iron and soldiers,' and saw in a turbulent and vindictive generation the aspiring children of Liberty. Mrs. Barbauld wrote of the island,

[5] Stendhal, *Vie de Napoléon*, I.

Liberty,
The mountain goddess, loves to range at large
Amid such scenes, and on the iron soil
Prints her majestic step.

To such the Corsicans were the modern Lacede-
monians, the sons of Nature, the disciples of
asceticism. The poet proclaims that they are
'true to their high descent,' which is from no less
a stock than 'Sparta's sad remains.' The British,
in particular, were fond of comparing Corsica to
their own island,

By nature destined the retreat of peace
And smiling Freedom; like Britannia, girt
With guardian waves; thy vales and watered
    plains
To persevering toil and culture yield
Abundance; not spontaneously profuse
To pamper sloth, but fertile to reward
The arts of industry.[6]

Rousseau, however, would not promise fame
to the Corsicans, but only happiness; he under-
stood very well that his system was one of re-
nunciation:

La nation ne sera point illustre, mais elle sera
heureuse. On ne parlera pas d'elle; elle aura
peu de considération au dehors; mais elle aura
l'abondance, la paix et la liberté dans son sein.

6 From *Corsica, a Poetical Address*, Glasgow, 1769. Anonymous.

In this land of peace and liberty there was to be the most careful regulation of marriage. A man who married before the age of twenty, or who married a girl less than fifteen, or a widow whose age differed from his own by more than twenty years, was to lose his citizenship. No bachelor was permitted to make a will or otherwise dispose of his property. All was confiscate to the state. Any bachelor who remained unmarried until the age of forty was to lose his rights of citizenship in perpetuity. On the other hand, a young woman who mated with a Corsican was to be dowered by the state, but only with land; of this, however, there was to be enough to enable the man, by industry, to rise to the primary rank of citizenship. If a man had more than five children, the state was to assist in supporting the sixth child and all subsequent children; but only resident offspring might be counted, and those absent from the island for more than a year might never be reckoned as belonging to the family, whether or not they returned. This last provision was aimed at the evil of depopulation, which, we have seen, had been assigned by many as one of the great causes of modern degeneracy.

Such are some of the provisions which Rousseau made for the ideal state. The system was never completed, and the experiment never tried.

Corsica was at the moment in a state of insurrection against her sovereign mistress, the republic of Genoa. Corsica had been in such a state, time out of mind. But her affairs were now rapidly approaching a climax, and it seemed as though she might succeed in gaining her independence from Genoa, and in establishing a republic which the powers would be able to recognise. There was already a provisional government, at the head of which was the Generalissimo of the Corsican armies, Pasquale Paoli, perhaps the greatest man that the island had yet produced. A man of noble ideals and gentle manners, he had united the factions of the island, guided their destinies with a firm hand, and enabled his people to make head against their enemies. By all representatives of liberal thought in Europe, except perhaps by Rousseau himself, who feared that in the new order of things, Paoli might not be willing to sink into the rôle of citizen-farmer, he was regarded not only as the founder of a new race—an Aeneas, a Lycurgus, an Epaminondas, a Solon, the father and legislator of his people—but also as the symbol and the morning star of a new era. Believers in the new theories of the rights of men, visionaries, and doctrinaires, turned eyes of hope and patient scrutiny towards Corsica and Paoli. When later

Paoli crossed the Continent, an admirer wrote:
'In Holland the Prince Statholder did him all
the honours in his power; and the Dutch seemed,
in his presence, to recover their ancient spirit
by which they threw off the Spanish yoke. He
passed through the Belgic hemisphere like a
planet of Liberty, warming every soul in his
progress.'[7] The name of a town in Pennsylvania
commemorates the interest which was felt in the
Corsican patriot by the colonists of America. To
Paoli, after the ruin of the Corsican hopes, Vittorio Alfieri dedicated *Timoleone,* his 'tragedy
of liberty,' as to one who, even in the degenerate
days of eighteenth century Italy, would be able
to read the tragedy aright.

In Corsica itself Paoli's authority was at a far
remove from the simplicities of the eighteenth
century system-makers. Burnaby found Paoli's
power unlimited, and says it was high treason
even to speak against him. 'Lo! a species of
despotism,' he adds, 'founded contrary to the
principles of Montesquieu upon love and affec-
tion.' Boswell found the devotion to the generalissimo so ardent that he was regarded as
'above humanity.' It was commonly believed
that he would in time extend the Corsican con-

[7] From an anonymous pamphlet, *A Review of the Conduct of
Pascal Paoli,* London, 1770.

quests beyond the limits of the island. He had
already captured the island of Capraja, and he
was expected to make a descent on Genoa itself.
He was revered by his people for his founding of
a university at Corte, as well as for his attention
to the humbler needs of the community in his in-
troduction of the potato. But in all his manifold
activity there was no suggestion of such a confi-
dence in his people as would lead him to the adop-
tion of the views of a Rousseau. In this, as in
other familiar instances, the radical theories
were the offspring of the philosopher and doc-
trinaire, not of the experienced statesman.

But Rousseau was not the only person who
devised a system of government for Corsica.
Mrs. Catharine Macaulay, Johnson's 'republi-
can' friend, whom Horace Walpole called 'a
brood-hen of faction,' addressed a pamphlet to
Paoli, entitled *A Short Sketch of a Democratical Form of Government.*[8] Long ere this she had
boldly declared that all forms of government
which have been 'imposed on credulous man'
have been defective, since they have not established the 'full and impartial security of the
rights of nature,' but have been rather 'formid-

8 London, 1767; it is a portion of a larger pamphlet entitled,
*Loose Remarks on Mr. Hobbes's Philosophical Rudiments of Gov-
ernment.*

able and dangerous cabals against the peace, happiness and dignity of society."[9] In her epistle to Paoli she asserted that any system of dependence was destructive of the virtues inherent in mankind. The 'democratical' form of a republic is the only system that can hope to shun this peril. Mrs. Macaulay explains to the General that she has studied 'free establishments' with care, and it is clear that she feels competent to construct the ideal government of the free. The plan, which is less extreme than that of Rousseau, need not detain us, save to mention her proposal, set down almost in so many words, that the government of Corsica ought to consist of a senate and a house of representatives, the make-up of which should be changed, by gradual degrees, every three years, so as to avoid the development of any privileged or governing class.

What Paoli thought of such theories of government it would be interesting to know. I am not aware that he ever paid any attention to Mrs. Macaulay; but he certainly wrote a letter to say that he would be glad to have Rousseau come to the island, and he certainly gave Buttafuoco permission to use his name in requesting Rousseau to draw up the constitution which has been de-

[9] *Observations on 'Thoughts on the Present Discontents,'* London, 1770; p. 8.

scribed. But there is not the slightest reason to suppose that he would have regarded himself as bound by any such documents. Paoli had everything to gain, not by securing ideal constitutions from European philosophers, but by drawing the attention of European authors and statesmen to the present condition of his island. He seems to have said something of the kind to Andrew Burnaby who visited the island in 1766, and who wrote:

I am persuaded that General Paoli had no intention, when he sent an invitation to Monsieur Rousseau, to suffer him, an entire stranger to the country, the people, the customs, and almost everything necessary to be known by a legislator, to form an ideal system of laws and then impose them upon the people. He was aware of the impropriety of this on several accounts; principally on that of their not being in a state ripe for the reception of any entire code of laws, whatsoever. He knew that their manners were to be greatly changed before they could be brought to such a temperament; that they were to be prepared gradually; were to be formed first for one law, then for another; each separate law laying a foundation for some future one, and by these means to be brought imperceptibly to the point he was desirous of. All he proposed from the presence of Rousseau was to avail himself of any hints he might be able to furnish him with; and that he might farther have the use of his pen to describe those many great and heroic actions which have been performed by the Corsicans, and which none but the pen of a Rousseau seems worthy of describing.[10]

But the most famous of all visitors to the island was James Boswell. Although he tells us that he had heard of Corsica ever since he was a boy, he probably had no great interest in Corsica until his visit to Rousseau. This occurred just at the close of the year 1764, at the moment when the philosopher was meditating on the laws which he would draw up for the new nation. He filled Boswell with admiration for the brave islanders, and fired his imagination with descriptions of Corsica as the cradle of liberty. The first word in the *Account of Corsica,* which Boswell put forth three years after his visit, is *liberty.* Liberty, he says, is indispensably necessary to our happiness, whether as individuals or as members of society. Indeed, 'everything worthy arises from it.' When he came into the presence of Paoli, he paid him a compliment which would have been fulsome, had it not expressed the settled conviction of liberal Europe: 'Sir, I am upon my travels, and have lately visited Rome.

[10] *Journal of a Tour to Corsica in the year 1766,* by the Revd. A. Burnaby. London, 1804.

I am come from seeing the ruins of one brave and free people: I now see the rise of another.'

Boswell was the first Briton to visit Corsica. His impudence in presenting himself, at the age of twenty-five, to General Paoli has been more often dwelt upon than his intrepidity in going to the island at all. About the same time, Rousseau confesses, he himself was deterred from going among the Corsicans by the frightful accounts which he received of the people. But Boswell, who was somewhat bored by his study of antiquities in Italy, desired to do and see something unique during his travels, and was not to be deterred. He proceeded to Corsica, then, in the autumn of 1765, during a lull in the fighting and at a time when the Genoese had been all but driven out of the island. A few towns had been garrisoned by French troops, but the French had promised to limit their occupancy to four years. There were, at the moment, therefore, no hostilities; nevertheless there was grave danger of Boswell's being mistaken for a spy, for the future was still uncertain. Indeed, as Paoli later told Fanny Burney,[11] he was at first convinced that Boswell was a spy, (or, as he pronounced the word, *an espy*), because the young fellow at once began taking notes of his conversation. When

[11]*Diary of Mme. D'Arblay,* October 15, 1782.

this unhappy delusion was dispelled, Paoli made much of his visitor. Perhaps he thought him a person of more distinction and power than was really the case; perhaps since he had failed to draw Rousseau to the island, he was fain to put up with this young Scotsman as a substitute, and get what advertisement and influence he could in England through him; but, however all this be, certain it is that the two became fast friends. It was for no merely international reasons that the General placed Boswell next him at dinner, permitted him to ride on his own horse with its trappings of crimson and gold, and presented him with his own pistols. Boswell himself says that the attention shown him as a subject of Great Britain was noised abroad in Italy and confirmed the notion that he was an envoy. The peasants and soldiers called him the *ambasciadore inglese.*

But though Boswell was not an English envoy to Corsica, he did his best to act the part of Corsican envoy to England when he returned. Paoli well knew that Boswell intended to plead the Corsican cause. 'When I asked him what I could possibly do in return for all his goodness to me, he replied, *Solamente disingannate il suo corte.* Only undeceive your court. Tell them what you have seen here. They will be curious to ask you. A man come from Corsica will be like

fair
sti

heu

J. Wale delt.   J. Miller Sc.

JAMES BOSWELL Esq.r

In the Dress of an Armed Corsican Chief, as he appear'd at
Shakespeare's Jubilee, at Stratford upon Avon September 1769.

a man come from the Antipodes. I expressed such hopes as a man of sensibility would in my situation naturally form. He saw at least one Briton devoted to his cause. I threw out many flattering ideas of future political events, imaged the British and the Corsicans strictly united both in commerce and in war, and described the blunt kindness and admiration with which the hearty, generous common people of England would treat the brave Corsicans.'

It has been customary among critics to laugh at Boswell's efforts on behalf of Corsica as a specimen of his characteristic presumption. His efforts have indeed their comic aspect, and it is, moreover, clear that in all his activity he was more than willing to acquire a personal renown as 'James Boswell, Esq., the Corsican traveller.' What traveller has not exaggerated the significance of his journeyings? And yet, when due allowance has been made for all this, there remain a generous devotion to a cause and an eagerness to serve a friend which it would be both foolish and cynical to deny. Boswell very ardently wished the success of the Corsican cause, and proposed to do what he could to promote it.

He took back with him a suit of Corsican attire by means of which he hoped to stimulate public interest and to call attention to himself. He

contrived to get a friend to present him to the
Prime Minister, and actually called on Lord
Chatham, wearing this Corsican costume. He
had much to say on behalf of Paoli to the Prime
Minister. Had not Paoli called Chatham the
Pericles of Great Britain? Could not Great
Britain save Corsica by a nod of the ministerial
head? This interview was a success—at least
Boswell was pleased with it—and a remark about
Paoli made by the Minister was carefully treas-
ured: 'It may be said of Paoli as the Cardinal
de Retz said of the great Montrose, "C'est un de
ces hommes qu'on ne trouve plus que dans les
Vies de Plutarque." '

Boswell wore this same costume when he went
to the Shakesperian jubilee at Stratford in the
autumn of 1769. He published an account of the
festivities in the *London Magazine,* together
with a print of himself wearing this now famous
costume. The account which accompanies it
contains the following paragraph:

Of the most remarkable masks upon this occasion was James Boswell, Esqr., in the dress of
an armed Corsican chief. He entered the amphi-
theatre about twelve o'clock. On the front of his
cap was embroidered in gold letters, *Viva la
Libertà,*—and on one side of it was a handsome
blue feather and cockade, so that it had an ele-

gant as well as a warlike appearance. He wore
no mask, saying that it was not proper for a gallant Corsican. So soon as he came into the
room, he drew universal attention.

In Ireland, whither he went a-wooing in the
spring of 1769, he had laid the cause of the Corsicans before the Lord Lieutenant, and had made
many friends for the 'gallant islanders.' Let us
hope that on this occasion, too, he wore his costume.

But his aid was also of a highly practical sort.
He raised a subscription of £700 in Scotland,[12]
and purchased ordnance of the Carron Company
for shipment to Corsica. Besides his *Account of
Corsica,* which included his *Journal of a Tour to
Corsica,* he superintended the collection and publication of a series of essays, entitled *British Es-*

[12] The following letter to the *Gentleman's Magazine* for November, 1768, is almost certainly by Boswell, bearing on its face the
mark of his familiar style. He was fond of addressing letters to
the magazine.
Mr. Urban,
 The generosity of his grace the Duke of Devonshire, Lord
Algernon Piercy, and Sir Watkins Williams Wynne, now on their
travels at Florence, in favour of the deserted Corsicans, deserves
a place in your valuable Magazine; these young travellers, on the
first news of the French invasion, remitted to Paoli the sum of
2000 l. each, by which seasonable supply he has been enabled to
make those brave efforts for the preservation of the liberty of
his country that have astounded all Europe.
                                                    E. Y.
 P.S. It is remarkable that among the lovers of liberty in
Scotland contributions have been raised for the brave Corsicans,
while in England the people have only wished their success.

says in behalf of the Brave Corsicans, by several hands.[13] These were all directed to a very practical end, British intervention to save Corsica from being swallowed up by France. The engraved frontispiece shows an allegorical figure of Corsica, accompanied by a dog, the symbol of fidelity, fleeing to Britannia for protection from France, who pursues her in a menacing attitude. This frontispiece is the redeeming feature in a very dull volume. There is much in the book about the rights of man and Corsica as the fortress of liberty, but the mark of 'propaganda' is upon the essays one and all, so that they can hardly lay claim to any literary character whatsoever. Inasmuch as it was necessary to publish the volume anonymously, as voicing the mind of a large though unidentified public, it necessarily lacked that personal touch which distinguishes everything else that Boswell ever wrote, and which makes even his proof-corrections delightful reading.

It was necessary, if anything were to be done for Corsica, to act and act quickly. England decided not to act. The cause of Corsican independence was lost for ever and the French ob-

[13] So far as I know, no effort has been made to discover the authorship of these various essays. Most of them, I fear, were from Boswell's own hand, although his friend Sir Alexander Dick and one or two others certainly lent assistance.

tained a foothold in the Mediterranean. It had
been necessary for Genoa to appeal for aid to
France, and the negotiations ended by the treaty
of 1769, in which Genoa ceded the island to the
crown of France. For a time Paoli struggled;
but sank at last under the enormous superiority
of the enemy. The neutrality of the British became a theme for scornful liberals. 'Sympathy
for Corsica,' writes G. O. Trevelyan,[14] 'was as
much the fashion with the English Whigs as
sympathy for America became seven years later,
among the more enlightened members of the
French nobility. . . . The theory that British
interests would suffer by our acquiescence in the
subjugation of Corsica—a theory backed by the
high authority of Frederick the Great—was
warmly urged by Shelburne in the Cabinet, and
would have prevailed but for the strenuous oppo-
sition of the Bedfords.'

Great was the dismay when it was learned that
the Government proposed to leave Corsica to her
fate. Many regarded it as a new indication of
the fatal luxury of the times. The anonymous
poet who printed *Corsica, a Poetical Address*, in
1769, attributed the base neutrality to

'The lust of power, the sordid thirst of gain,'

[14] *Early History of C. J. Fox,* chap. IV.

as well as to 'pleasure's poisonous draught.'
England was disinclined to go to war. 'Foolish
as we are,' said Lord Holland, 'we cannot be so
foolish as to go to war because Mr. Boswell has
been in Corsica, and yet, believe me, no better
reason can be given for siding with the vile inhabitants of one of the vilest islands in the world,
who are not less free than all the rest of their
neighbours, and whose island will enable the
French to do no more harm than they may do us
at any time from Toulon.'[15]

The British received Paoli with all cordiality
when he came as a refugee to London. The king
granted him an audience, and a pension of a
thousand a year from the exchequer. Paoli seems
to have reconciled himself to life in England,
which Boswell took care to make delightful for
him. He resided in London for the next twenty
years, until the French Revolution brought him
once more to political prominence. Corsica, too,
consented to live, though the threat had been
made that she would shed every drop of her dear
blood before she would consent to be again a
slave. Peace doth recant vows made in war. In
time Corsica was able to console herself for her
slavery by producing a man who was to reign as
emperor over these French enslavers; for one of

[15] From G. O. Trevelyan's *Early History of Fox*, chap. IV.

the indirect results of the sale of the island to France was that Napoleon Bonaparte was born a French citizen. Baron Stendhal places near the beginning of his *Life of Napoleon* a comparison of Paoli and Bonaparte. 'Paoli,' he says, 'fut comme le type et l'image de toute la vie future de Napoléon.'

But all this is far from our theme. The grief that followed the collapse of the Corsican hopes was more than that occasioned by the mere defeat of a gallant little people. The generous-minded had looked to Corsica as something more than a group of patriots desirous of changing their form of government. It had been more than a republic that was being founded; it was an ideal that was being put into a world of reality, a hope that burned in the minds of men, a belief that it might yet be possible to purify the hearts and moderate the passions of mankind, until brotherly love should replace national rivalries, and put an end to war. *Liberty, equality, fraternity*—the words are commonplace and tawdry enough to-day; but in 1769 they were, at least in their practical application to the life of nations, as fresh as an April dawn and as full of promise. The promise faded and the hope decayed; only to revive in the next decade—in a form which needs no reference here. But, for the

moment, hearts were embittered, for boundless
had been the hopes of what mankind might
accomplish in a state of freedom. And now the
spirit of man had made its great refusal. It was
not to be released from the 'meagre, stale, forbid-
ding ways of custom, law, and statute.' It had
failed in the testing hour.

And with these high hopes fell the belief that
a new era had opened for poetry and the arts.
The dawn had seemed to be breaking. The sons
of a rugged island had risen in native, God-cre-
ated majesty, and soon might be expected to sing
a new song to the world.

> Th' immortal Muse,
> Fired by the voice of Freedom, soars sublime,

said the poet of Corsica. Miss Aikin, too, had
felt the fire of prophecy descend upon her:

> Then shall the shepherd's pipe, the muse's
>   lyre,
> On Cyrnus' shores be heard. Her grateful
>   sons
> With loud acclaim and hymns of cordial
>   praise
> Shall hail their high deliverers.

Paoli himself had not been untouched by some
of these high hopes, for he told Boswell that arts
and sciences were not to be expected from Corsica at once; but that in twenty or thirty years'

time, the island would be able to display them.—
But now the dream was over, and Corsica had
sunk back into slavery.

Corsica may, perhaps, have been in the mind
of Boswell on those numerous occasions when he
led Johnson to talk about the nature of government. High hopes of social regeneration were
no characteristic of Johnson's Tory soul, and he
enjoined Boswell to clear his head of Corsica.
As for himself, he would not give half a guinea
to live under one form of government rather than
another.

It would be an agreeable shifting of responsi-
bility if we could adopt the theory that human
happiness and a florescence of the arts depend
upon the form of government under which we
live.

In every government, though terrors reign,
Though tyrant kings or tyrant laws restrain,
How small, of all that human hearts endure,
That part which laws or king can cause or
    cure.

A poet may of course be less contented under
one form of government than another, and the
public indifference to his art may receive point
and emphasis from the indifference of king or
minister; but it is difficult to discover what all
this coldness has to do with the poet's singing

voice. A government can neither bestow that nor take it away. When all else fails, when patrons betray and the guardians of the public trust capitulate, when virtue goes over to the world and truth is crushed to earth, it is the poet's hour. Let him sing of his broken heart.

Upon this subject Lord Chesterfield had expressed himself with characteristic sanity some years before. His words, though not eloquent, have a certain value, especially as coming from one who was generally regarded as belonging to the old order of things:

It is a general prejudice and has been propagated for these sixteen hundred years that arts and sciences cannot flourish under an absolute government, and that genius must necessarily be cramped where freedom is restrained. This sounds plausible, but is false in fact. Mechanic arts, as agriculture, manufactures, etc., will indeed be discouraged where the profits and property are, from the nature of a government, insecure. But why the despotism of a government should cramp the genius of a mathematician, an astronomer, a poet, or an orator, I confess I never could discover. It may indeed deprive the poet or the orator of the liberty of treating certain subjects in the manner they would wish; but it leaves them subjects enough to exert genius upon, if they have it.[16]

[16] *Letters to his Son*, February 7, 1749.

What, pray, was to prevent the Corsicans from singing,—except, indeed, a lack of bards? If there had been potential singers, ready to break into song in the hour of victory, why might they not, with garland and singing robes about them, have grown lyrical upon the subject of their wrongs?

Most wretched men are cradled into poetry
   by wrong:
They learn in suffering what they teach in
   song.

A rebirth of poetry was to occur in England in the next decade, that of the 'eighties. It saw the emergence of William Cowper and William Blake, of George Crabbe and Robert Burns. Think for a moment whether the reign of George III, which we of America have been prone to describe as tyrannous, exercised any chilling or restraining influence upon these men. Can it, on the other hand, be said to account for their inspiration? None of them was perhaps wholly uninterested in the government under which he lived; but none of them, so far as I am aware, dreamed of awaiting the perfection of that government before beginning to sing. Two of them became passionately interested in the French Revolution (which has long done service in accounting for the inspiration of English

poets); but the Revolution was undreamed of
when these men made their definitive appearance
in the poetic world. Three of the poets sang in
spite of a poverty bitter enough to have chilled the
ardour of any man; and the fourth spoke from a
heart heavy with the dread of approaching mad-
ness. And yet, in spite of all the wrong and the
woe which they knew so well, they were the her-
alds of the dawn, the symbols of a new order.
But the explanation of their representative position is not found in either the restraint or the
extension of their personal liberty or that of the
nation to which they belonged; for the dayspring
of poetry, whether it appear in Corsica or in
England, in Paris or in Princeton, is from on
high.

III

ANCIENT BARD AND GENTLE SAVAGE

But heed, ye bards, that for the sign of onset
Ye sound the antientest of all your rhymes,
Whose birth Tradition notes not, nor who fram'd
Its lofty strains.

—Mason, *Caractacus.*

The leading English poet of the mid-eighteenth century, the man who was most tremulously responsive to its changing manner and enlarging thought, lived in almost complete retirement from the world. To his contemporaries Thomas Gray must have seemed detached from everything that could reveal the true literary movement of the day—a fatally isolated and academic figure. In 1750 he had finally published, after incredible elaboration, a poem which became at once the most popular in the language, the famous *Elegy.* But of all poets then living Gray was perhaps the least fitted to enjoy the prominence and popularity which he had achieved; he was not only shy, but like most shy people, somewhat cynical as well, hurt by censure yet uncon-

61

vinced by praise, self-conscious when he should have been self-assertive, and with a large contempt for the vulgar, even when they united in his praise. Any other poet than Gray would have been profoundly influenced by the success of the *Elegy;* it would have fixed the character of his literary production for many years. But Gray never made a second attempt. His eager and changeful interests had passed on to a type of poetry as different from the *Elegy* as may easily be conceived. Four years after the production of his masterpiece he began the composition, in his hesitant fashion, of two Pindaric odes, cast, to be sure in an antique mould, but filled with new themes, and in the most remarkable manner prophetic of the literary movement of the next two decades. It has long been common to remark that in Gray's poetry we have an epitome of that of his age. This reputation, surprising enough for a poet so essentially academic as Gray, is the more unusual because of his lack of one of the fundamental poetic qualities. Gray lacked passion, and he knew it. He was by nature pensive, melancholy, scholastic; there was none of that 'wild dedication of himself' so characteristic of romanticism. Poetry needed, he knew, not only 'the master's hand,' which was already his, but

'the prophet's fire,' which was by no means his.
This lack he felt not only in himself, but, quite
properly, in the poetry (so-called) which was being produced all about him.[1] The more he dwelt
upon the lack, the more he came to feel that this
prophetic fire which had deserted poetry had once
been its most characteristic sign, and had, indeed, inspired the very origins of the art. The
farther back one went in poetic history, the more
intense was this passionate utterance, which now
the age had lost. Therefore, for the Pindaric
odes, he selected subjects which permitted him to
return, at least in imagination, to the intenser
passion of these earlier ages; perhaps they would
touch his lips as with a living coal. The *Progress of Poesy* is a typically eighteenth century
theme, in which the tradition of poetry is followed from ancient Greece down to Thomas
Gray himself, but the poem contains very remarkable novelties and, if not passion, at least

[1] But not to one in this benighted age
   Is that diviner inspiration giv'n
 That burns in Shakespeare's or in Milton's page—
   The pomp and prodigality of heav'n.
In his essay on Lydgate, Gray says:
 'I fear the quickness and the delicate impatience of these pol-
ished times in which we live are but the forerunners of the de-
cline of all those beautiful arts which depend upon the imagina-
tion.' He uses both 'pomp' and 'imagination' of the Ossianic
poetry (*infra*, p. 66).

more abandon than Gray had yet permitted himself.

I desire in particular to direct your attention to one of the stanzas which is conspicuous for its romantic subject-matter:

> In climes beyond the solar road,
> Where shaggy forms o'er ice-built mountains roam,
> The Muse has broke the twilight gloom
>   To chear the shiv'ring Native's dull
>   abode.
> And oft, beneath the od'rous shade
> Of Chili's boundless forests laid,
> She deigns to hear the savage Youth repeat
> In loose numbers wildly sweet
>   Their feather-cinctured chiefs and
>   dusky loves.

Lapland and Chili in 1754! All this, we may well remind ourselves, is nearly twenty years before that renewal of interest in primitive man which ensued upon the explorations of the 'sixties, and which was discussed in the first of these lectures. But Gray's digest of the passage in the annotations makes it still more worthy of analysis. 'Extensive influence of poetic genius over the remotest and most uncivilised nations: its connection with liberty and the virtues that naturally attend on it.' Liberty, it appears, therefore, is as much the need of poetry as of nations. In particular Liberty brings into poetry romantic passion (since the verse is to be 'wildly sweet') and 'loose numbers.' Liberty is opposed to the restraints of society, the inhibitions of culture, and encourages that wild dedication of oneself to dusky love and feather-cinctured chief, which lends a vivid passion to the verses. And the 'loose numbers'?—or, translating into French, shall we say *vers libres*? Clearly, the poetry of the Chilian savage boy will not be in the Pindaric form! Perhaps it will be found not to respect the bonds of metre, but to pour its ecstasy in some lawless though eloquent mode, while Liberty stands smiling by. Perhaps, our poet may have felt, the language of passion is inconsistent with the regular harmonies and fixed rhythm of eighteenth century verse. Poets were abandoning the heroic couplet for blank verse, for 'ode and elegy, and sonnet'; would a perfect obedience to the law of Liberty compel them to abandon metre entirely?

Gray's other Pindaric ode, *The Bard,* is, by common consent, the more romantic of the two. I will not analyse so familiar a poem, but only point out that in it we encounter, as the poet's chief creation, the figure of the ancient bard himself. The author no longer writes about primitive song, but gives us the primitive singer.

There he stands upon the slopes of Snowdon, and sings forth the story of his woe, while the cruel troops of Edward I pass through the valley at his feet.

A few years later, under the influence of Ossian, Gray wrote, as though summarising all his earlier views: 'Imagination dwelt many hundred years ago in all her pomp on the cold and barren mountains of Scotland. The truth (I believe) is that, without respect of climates, she reigns in all nascent societies of men, where the necessities of life force everyone to think and act much for himself.'[2]

This theory of Gray's was amusingly set forth in Lloyd and Colman's burlesque of *The Bard:*

> Shall not applauding critics hail the vogue?
> Whether the Muse the style of Cambria's sons,
> Or the rude gabble of the Huns,
>   Or the broader dialect
>   Of Caledonia she affect,
> Or take, Hibernia, thy still ranker brogue?

With Gray's these satirists coupled the name of a contemporary poet and dear friend, William Mason, who is still remembered for two verse-tragedies in the Greek style, *Elfrida* and *Caractacus*. The second of them is closely connected with the present subject because it was

[2] Gray to Brown, February 8, 1763.

composed under the influence of Gray and with his careful assistance and criticism. Indeed, the drama itself is plainly inspired by *The Bard;* only instead of a single minstrel, with harp and streaming beard, we have a whole chorus of them, who sing strophic odes antiphonally, and comment on the action of the piece after the manner of the chorus in a Greek tragedy. The life of these minstrels is well described by one of the characters of the drama:

> Yonder grots
> Are tenanted by bards, who nightly thence,
> Robed in their flowing vests of innocent white,
> Descend with harps that glitter to the moon,
> Hymning immortal strains.

The subject of this tragedy is the betrayal and capture of Caractacus, the aged British leader, and the slaughter in battle of Arviragus, his only son, the great general of the Britons. Arviragus is himself, one of the tribe of heroic savages; except for colour, he is cousin-german to Oroonoko, for he is animated by all the generous impulses and nobility of soul that distinguish the genus. The action of the piece passes in the sacred grove of the Druids, in the midst of which stands an altar surrounded by a Druid circle of stones; there is the usual background of brawling stream, cliffs, and yawning chasms. The Principal

Druid speaks for the British nation, and his attendant bards sing the odes.

These lyrical passages are certainly the best poetry Mason ever wrote. Gray admired them intensely. They were afterwards excerpted from the drama, and made into an oratorio,[3] for which Dr. Arne wrote the music. Of the many odes which the play contains this is, perhaps, the best. It bears some slight resemblance to the lyrics in Byron's *Manfred:*

> Mona on Snowdon calls:
> Hear, thou king of mountains, hear;
> 　Hark, she speaks from all her strings;
> 　Hark, her loudest echo rings;
> King of mountains, lend thine ear,
> 　Send thy spirits, send them soon,
> 　Now when Midnight and the Moon
> Meet upon thy front of snow:
> 　See, their gold and ebon rod,
> 　Where the sober sisters nod,
> And greet in whispers sage and slow.
> Snowdon, mark!　'tis Magic's hour.

To the already numerous bards in our midst there is now added a further company of *phantom* bards:

> Snowdon has heard the strain:
> Hark, amid the wondering grove,
> 　Other harpings answer clear,

[3] *The Lyrical Part of Caractacus,* London, 1776.

Other voices meet our ear;
Pinions flutter, shadows move,
 Busy murmurs hum around,
 Rustling vestments brush the ground;
Round and round and round they go,
 Thro' the twilight, thro' the shade,
 Mount the oak's majestic head,
And gild the tufted mistletoe.
Cease ye glittering race of light,
Close your wings, and check your flight.
Here arranged in order due,
Spread your robes of saffron hue;
For lo, with more than mortal fire,
Mighty Mador smites the lyre:
Hark, he sweeps the master-strings.

Whatever you may think of Mason's verses, you
will observe that he has outdone Gray in
depicting the life of the bard, not of course because he has multiplied the number of singers,
but because he has aspired to show the bard at
what he conceived to be the bardic task of guid-
ing the destinies of a people. His was the 'master's hand, the prophet's fire' in ancient Britain.
The entire picture is highly idealised of course,
as are the 'loose numbers' of the bard, which
he often permits in

        unbridled course to rush
Thro' dissonance to concord, sweetest then
Ev'n when expected harshest.

Mason seems to have felt that he could best give
an impression of free verse by exchanging the
regularities of iambic rhythm for the continual
variations of the strophic ode. We are not of
course to assume that he supposed that the ancient bards actually sang anything like them.
The use of a strophic form was as far as Mason,
who was in no sense an original person, dared to
go. Gray had chosen this as the most fitting
modern medium for the bardic chant, and Mason
instinctively followed the lead of his master.
The real step in the direction of 'loose numbers'
was to be taken by Mason's successor who, abandoning fixed metres altogether, represented the
bard as singing rhythmic, or, if you will, polyphonic, prose.

The bardic figure had now reached a high de-
gree of imaginative development—so high, indeed, that a need was felt for something more
substantial than a poet's dream of what a bard
might have sung. Oh, for the song itself, the
very words of the minstrel of Nature, as he sang
them to the British warrior thirteen hundred
years ago!

And pat it came—just at the moment when
the public was prepared to receive it, in the line
of direct descent from Mason and from Gray—
the poems of Ossian, son of Fingal, ancient Brit-

FINGAL.

AN
ANCIENT EPIC POEM,

In SIX BOOKS:

Together with feveral other POEMS, compofed by

OSSIAN the Son of FINGAL.

Tranflated from the GALIC LANGUAGE,

By JAMES MACPHERSON.

Fortia facta patrum.   VIRGIL.

LONDON:

Printed for T. BECKET and P. A. DE HONDT, in the Strand.

M DCC LXII.

ish bard of the third century A.D., filled with the
prophet's fire, sung in loose numbers wildly
sweet, in honour of the chieftains of old, passionate, sad as the wind that sobbed over Morven,
the joy of heroes, the consolation of the bereaved.
The dream of Gray come true! The highly-
coloured imaginings of Mason outstripped by the
authentic facts of history! But *were* they authentic? *Caractacus* was published in the spring
of 1759, the first volume of Ossianic poetry in the
autumn of 1760. The sequence was suspicious.
Ossian, when one thought it all out in cool blood,
had come a little too pat. There is no necessity
of rehearsing here the well-known history of the
publication—within four short years—of the Ossianic epics and lyric fragments which are now
known to have been almost entirely the work of a
young Scots clergyman, James Macpherson,
with a gift for making vague sublimities moan
through polyphonic prose. On the title-page of
the epic, *Fingal* (Macpherson's second Ossianic
'discovery'), is a beautiful engraving of the bard
himself, exactly as the bard had been conceived
in the previous decade. The blind harper, clad
in flowing robes, 'with beard that rests on his
bosom,' sits before the caves and crags, already
dear to the romantic heart, and sings a tale of
the olden time.

The essential similarity between the creations
of Gray and of Macpherson is attested by the
immediate interest which the former poet took
in the Ossianic publications and his eagerness to
have their authenticity proved. In the end, he
seems to have accepted them as genuine.

No less important than the influence of Ossian
upon the literatures of Europe was the counter
effect of the bardic tradition in getting specimens
of genuinely primitive poetry brought to public
attention. *Temora,* the last of Macpherson's Ossianic forgeries, appeared in 1763, the same year
in which Percy put forth his *Five Pieces of
Runic Poetry from the Icelandic.* In the next
year Evan Evans published his *Specimens of the
Poetry of the Antient Welsh Bards,* which was
followed in 1765 by Percy's *Reliques of Ancient
English Poesy.* It is, perhaps, correct to say
that the Ossianic forgeries could have been successfully published only in the decade of the 'sixties; for ten years earlier there would have been
no demand for them, and ten years later too much
was known about the nature of early narrative
poetry—at least that of the north—to permit of
so general a hoax.

But what of the south? In *The Bard,* it will
be recalled, Gray described the Muse as listening

not only to the Icelandic or Lapland peasant, but also to the savage youth of the boundless forests of Chili. With this figure it was far more difficult to deal than with the ancient bard because there was a total lack of acquaintance with the religion, folk-lore, and customs of the Malay, the African, and the American. The idealisation of the redskin belongs to a later generation.[4] Smollett's description of the Indians in *Humphry Clinker* is the most extravagant burlesque —the humour of the comic supplement—except where, by way of sneering at the French Jesuits, he represents the Indian's religion of Nature as superior to Catholicism.

The negro was a somewhat more popular figure, though the full tide of sympathy was delayed for ten years or so. Nevertheless Dr.

[4] I have of course not attempted even a sketch of the long and fascinating history of the sentimentalised savage, whether red or black, Icelandic or Malay. I am concerned only with the sudden revival of interest in him which, as I have said before, is connected with the explorations of the eighteenth century navigators. To trace the origin of the idealised redskin would take one back at least to Lope da Vega, who in the second act of *El Nuevo Mundo* represents a group of Indians as singing an antiphonal chant to the Sun, which contains allusions to Phoebus and Diana. [This reference I owe to my friend Professor Stoll.] In England the tradition is at least as old as Florio.

The tendency to idealise the Indian was undoubtedly furthered by the missionaries who desired to put the Indian character in the best possible light.

Hawkesworth's version of *Oroonoko,* which revived, in a disinfected form, Southerne's old
tragedy, (which was itself a dramatisation of
Aphra Behn's novel), was acted in 1775 with
some success. In this the noble black man appeared in his usual rôle of ethical grandeur.
This version of Hawkesworth's contains, as an
addition of his own, a song supposed to be sung
by the slaves on a West Indian plantation. It
has, to be sure, a somewhat operatic ring about it.

> Come, let us be gay, to repine is in vain,
> When our loss we forget, what we lose we
>   retain;
> Our toils with the day are all ended at last;
> Let us drown in the present all thoughts of
>   the past,
> All the future commit to the Powers above
> Come, give us a smile as an earnest of Love.
>
> > Ah no—it will not, cannot be;
> > Love, Love, and Joy must still be free,
> > The toils of day indeed are past,
> > And gentle Evening comes at last;
> > But gentle Evening comes in vain
> > To soothe the slave from sense of pain.
>
> In vain the Song and Dance invite
> To lose reflection in delight;
> Thy voice thy anxious heart belies,
> I read thy bondage in thy eyes:
> Does not thy heart with mine agree?

Man.   Yes, Love and Joy must both
be free.
Woman.   Must both be free, for both disdain
The sounding scourge and gall-
ing chain.
Man.   'Tis true, alas! they both disdain
The sounding scourge and gall-
ing chain.

Interest in the passionate children of the south
was vastly heightened by the arrival in England
of Omai, or Omiah, a native of Ulitea (now
Raiatea), brought from the Society Islands by
Captain Furneaux in the autumn of 1774. Omai,
unlike the Esquimaux described in a previous
lecture, knew how to make himself agreeable to
the persons he met, and displayed an enthusiastic
appreciation of civilisation. Everyone who came
into contact with him seems to have liked him,
for he possessed what a contemporary called the
'unsuspecting good-nature of childhood,' a re-
spectful and even genteel manner, and a *naïve-
té* that delighted everybody. Omai's exact
age was not known, but he was somewhere in his
twenties. He is described as 'tawny,' with the
flat nose, and thick lips of the Polynesian. His
hands and fingers were tattooed. He had long
black hair flowing over his shoulders. His ex-

pression of countenance was intelligent, yet
placid and kindly.

Omai's portrait was drawn several times while
he was in England. The best picture of him is,
in my opinion, that of Nathaniel Dance, which
was engraved by the Bartolozzi in October, 1774.
Dance has not only indicated the sweet temper
of the savage, but has produced a picture of use
as a document and a record. Omai is shown with
his long hair loose over his shoulders, and with
tattoo-marks visible on his hands in which he holds
an Otaheitan stool or seat, a bag, and a fan. He
is arrayed in a long robe, elaborately wound
about his shoulders and waist, so as to cover his
body, with the exception of his forearms, feet,
and ankles, which are bare. This, I suppose, was
the contemporary notion of the way a savage
should be represented in art. His is certainly not
the Tahitan costume, of the simplicities of which
we are, perhaps, sufficiently informed, and which
would not serve in the rigors of a London
autumn; neither is it the costume which Omai
wore in England as a rule, for it was found more
convenient for him to don the conventional
clothes of the day; so he appeared regularly in a
reddish brown coat, white waistcoat, breeches,
and sword—a costume which pleased him and the
century well enough.

OMAI a Native of ULAIETEA.

OMAI.

From an engraving by Bartolozzi, after a drawing by Nathaniel Dance.

Sir Joshua Reynolds gives a different picture of Omai.[5] He was impressed by the dignity of the young savage, and therefore posed him in a heroic attitude against a fanciful Otaheitan land-scape, which is perhaps the first attempt in the history of English art to depict the scenery of Tahiti. He wears the flowing robes and also a turban. Every trace of barbarousness, except the bare feet, is carefully omitted by Reynolds, who has succeeded in lending to the Polynesian savage the poise and regal aloofness of an Arab. Nothing could reveal more adequately the traits which were sought for in the gentle savage. Yet Reynolds's picture is true to one side of Omai, for all the testimony with regard to him—and we have a great deal—constantly emphasizes his courtesy and self-restraint under the strange and difficult conditions into which he had been thrust. Boswell uses the word *elegance* to describe his be-haviour, and says that Johnson accounted for it on the ground that Omai had passed his time, while in England, only in the best company.[6] Mrs. Thrale invited Omai to her home at Streat-ham, where he was introduced to Johnson, who gave the following account to Boswell: 'Sir, Lord Mulgrave and he dined one day at Streat-

[5] See the frontispiece to this book.
[6] *Life*, Hill's ed., vol. 3, p. 8.

ham; they sat with their backs to the light fronting me, so that I could not see distinctly; and there was so little of the savage in Omai, that I was afraid to speak to either, lest I should mistake one for the other.'

Mrs. Thrale tells us that when Omai beat Baretti at chess, everybody admired the savage's good-breeding and the European's impatience— a subject on which Johnson delighted to tease Baretti.[7]

Omai passed a large part of his time with Lord and Lady Sandwich at Hinchinbroke, and there is said to have been woe in the heart of the peeress when the savage left her. Omai was presented at court, and given an allowance by George III, whom he addressed by the delightful and appropriate name of *King Tosh*.[8] The author of the anonymous satire entitled, *Omiah's Farewell, inscribed to the Ladies of London*,[9] calls Omai 'the courteous Indian,'[10] and asserts that 'the first personages of the kingdom' were 'assiduous to do him favours.' In truth, Omai developed a very real preference for fine society, and showed marked indifference to the lower

[7] Collison-Morley, *Baretti and his Friends*, p. 220 *et. seq.* Cf. Hill, *Johnsonian Miscellanies*, vol. 2, p. 292.

[8] *Tosh,* his attempt to pronounce 'George.'

[9] London, 1776.

[10] *i.e.*, 'Savage.'

classes, a characteristic which the enthusiastic believers in equality and fraternity among men in
a state of nature might have studied to their considerable enlightenment.

A very human and charming side of Omai is
revealed by George Colman in his *Random
Recollections.* Colman, when a little boy, met
Omai during an expedition of Sir Joseph Banks,
the botanist, who had gone into Yorkshire to
gather herbs. Omai, who was living with Banks
at the moment, took a fancy to 'Tosh,' as he called
the boy George. The savage and the youngster
went in swimming together, and Omai carried
George on his back, to his alternate fear and delight, for the boy had never been in the sea before. Omai entertained the whole party; gave an
exhibition of Otaheitan cooking; stalked a covey
of partridges and caught one in his hands—to the
horror of British sportsmanship; seized a gallop-
ing horse by the tail and allowed himself to be
dragged along by the terrified animal, while he
gave an exhibition of agility in shunning the
flying hoofs. He and the boy made up a lingo
for themselves, half Otaheitan, half English, in
which they contrived to jabber to their mutual
enlightenment. What boy could ask for a better companion?

Very little was done to improve Omai's mind

while he was in England. It was even roundly
asserted that Banks preferred to keep him in a
state of primitive ignorance as an object of curi-
osity.[11] Omai himself wished to learn to write,
but no steps were taken to teach him. He appears to have had no regular instruction after
leaving his first teacher, James Burney, who
could speak Otaheitan. He was obliged to 'pick
up' what English he could—with the usual de-
plorable results of that process. Nevertheless
his untutored efforts to express himself are more
interesting than any real mastery of the language
could have been, since they are at once pointed,
picturesque, and, often, adequate. Though they
convulsed people with laughter, they beautifully
illustrate the indebtedness of language to meta-
phor and, indeed, reveal the essentially poetic
mind of the savage. Ice, for example, which he
had never seen before, he called, appropriately
enough, *stone-water*.[12] Snow was similarly
'white rain.' He assumed that a person who used
snuff was satisfying an appetite, and therefore in
declining the offer of a pinch, said simply, 'No
tank you, Sir, me nose be no hungry.'[13] He even

[11] Sir Joseph Cullum's notes, first published by Edward Smith
in his *Life of Banks* (1911), p. 41.

[12] Walpole's *Letters*, January 28, 1776.

[13] *Cumberland Letters*, October 10, 1774.

experienced difficulty in referring to the familiar
domestic animals, since, as a Tahitan, the only
quadrupeds he knew were the hog, the dog, and
the rat.   Therefore he instinctively called a horse
a 'big hog.'   For a bull in a field he early acquired a respect, and referred, 'reverentially,' as
Colman puts it, to a 'man-cow.'

Fanny Burney, who thought that Omai's gra-
cious manner 'shamed Education,' and expatiated
on his greatness of soul, gives a good account of
his conversation[14] in all its strangeness.   She was
vastly amused at it, though she found it difficult
to understand.   She also had the privilege of
hearing Omai sing a native song, and though she
was not pleased, her account may be given in
full.   It may serve to bring us back to the subject of primitive poetry: ·

My father, who fortunately came in during his
visit, asked him very much to favour us with a
song of his own country, which he had heard him
sing at Hinchinbrooke.   He seemed to be quite
ashamed; but we all joined and made the request
so earnestly, that he could not refuse us.   But
he was either so modest, that he blushed for his
own performance, or his residence here had made
him so conscious of the *barbarity* of the South
Sea Islands' music, that he could hardly prevail
with himself to comply with our request; and

[14] *Early Diary*, 2.132.

when he did, he began two or three times, before he could acquire voice or firmness to go on.

Nothing can be more *curious* or less *pleasing* than his singing voice; he seems to have none; and *tune* or *air* hardly seem to be aimed at; so queer, wild, strange a *rumbling of sounds* never did I before hear; and very contentedly can I go to the grave, if I never do again. His *song* is the only thing that is *savage* belonging to him.

The *story* that the words told, was laughable enough, for he took great pains to explain to us *the English* of the song. It appeared to be a sort of *trio* between an old woman, a young woman, and a young man. The two latter are entertaining each other with praises of their merits and protestations of their passions, when the old woman enters, and endeavours to *faire l'aimable* to the youth; but, as she cannot boast of her *charms,* she is very earnest in displaying her *dress,* and making him observe and admire her taste and fancy. Omiah, who stood up to *act* the scene, was extremely droll and diverting by the grimaces, *minauderies,* and affectation he assumed for this character, examining and regarding himself and his dress with the most conceited self-complacency. The youth then avows his passion for the nymph; the old woman sends her away, and, to use Omiah's own words, coming forward to offer *herself,* says, 'Come! *marry me!*' The young man starts as if he had seen a viper, then makes her a bow, begs to be excused, and runs off.

Though the singing of Omy is so barbarous, his actions, the expression he gives to each character, are so original and so diverting, that they did not fail to afford us very great entertainment of the *risible* kind.

Now anyone experienced in the collection of folk-lore could have explained to Fanny and her father that they had gone about their business in a singularly unhappy way. They had first made the singer self-conscious, and had then permitted him to apologise for the *barbarity* of his song. Just what effect Omai expected to produce I of course, cannot say; but I feel certain that, during the singing, the Burney girls must frequently have been giggling—or choking down their giggles—when they should have found something of a truly serious import. In short, if Miss Burney despised Omai's song, it was because she did not know how to listen to it. She was a true daughter of the century. Had Omai sung in a minor key something vaguely sublime and wildly passionate—had he somehow or other happened to recall Ossian to her mind—she would have been transported with delight. But there was no hint of the heroic in what he sang— no note of primitive passion. He was not the minstrel of the tropics singing of dusky loves and feather-cinctured chiefs, and his piece was in no way like *The Bard* or the odes of Mason. It was something quite different in kind from the poetry that Miss Burney knew, something that had to be explained to her, something queer and grotesque, like the decorations on an Indian pot, of which, naturally, she had never heard. But the loose numbers, the wild sweetness, the bursting heart, the rude eloquence of Nature—these were not in it, for these things belong to romanticism, and not to primitive poetry.

The little scrap of folk-lore from the South Seas which found its final resting-place in the vivacious diary of Miss Burney bears upon it several of the characteristic marks of primitive poetry. It blends poetry, music, and dramatic action into a single product, in which no one of the three component elements is quite distinguishable from the others. The acting and the grimaces of Omai, we may be sure, were not assumed for the mere purpose of making his song intelligible to the company, but were vitally necessary to the piece as he had received it from tradition.

When Banks was first in Tahiti, he heard some native songs,[15] which he must have considered trivial enough, since he did not take the trouble to record them:

[15] Journal, June 12, 1769.

'There was a large concourse of people round
the band, which consisted of two flutes and three
drums, the drummers accompanying their music
with their voices. They sang many songs, generally in praise of us, for these gentlemen, like
Homer of old, must be poets as well as musi-
cians.'

It would be interesting to know what the Polynesian Homer sang when first the white shadows appeared in the South Seas. Banks was not
sufficiently interested to find out and write down
even the verses about himself, but was content
to record that the songs were short and not without rime and metre. Such songs are frequently
improvisatorial and close to the event or person
that they celebrate or describe. Had the poetry
been recorded for us, we should have found it
simple indeed, and its singers untutored; but we
should not have found it easy to understand or
valuable as a model. Indeed it could not have
been successfully imitated, any more than Dr.
Burney, with all his music, could have blown a
tune on an Otaheitan flute. All imitation of
primitive verse is a *tour de force*. It may be,
like one of Chatterton's Rowley poems or one of
Rossetti's imitations of a popular ballad, ex-
ceedingly beautiful; but it is a new thing with
qualities of its own and of its age. The fabrica-

tions of Macpherson and his disciple Chatterton
have no doubt their own peculiar charm, but it
is not the charm of the centuries which they pro-
fess, respectively, to represent.

Before the movement had spent itself, there
arose a poet in England who united much of the
new romantic fashions of his day with the common sense, the chilly and prosaic sense, that had
long characterised the age. This was William
Cowper. He himself had written a poem in
which an ancient bard was represented as speaking to Queen Boadicea

> prophetic words
> Pregnant with celestial fire,
>   Bending as he swept the chords
> Of his sweet but awful lyre.

He felt and gave poetic expression to the new
emotions about mankind and the equally new
emotions about animals. He felt pity for poor
Africans shut up in the hold of a slave-trader
and pity for poor prisoners shut up in the Bas-
tille. Yet he never really surrendered himself to
the ecstasies of romanticism, and therefore in his
lines of farewell to Omai, (for after a year or
two, the courteous savage was taken back to the
Society Islands), Cowper displays that sanity
and that calmness which have been so noticeably

absent from all the utterances regarding primi-
tivism which we have studied. The lines are, like
much that Cowper wrote, prim and drab, but not
without a certain interest to those who have followed Omai's career. He is speaking—indeed,
Cowper is usually speaking—of life in the country.[16]

Here virtue thrives as in her proper soil;
Not rude and surly and beset with thorns,
And terrible to sight as when she springs
(If e'er she springs spontaneous) in remote
And barbarous climes, where violence prevails
And strength is lord of all . . .
War and the chase engross the savage whole.

The man who wrote those lines had not forgotten the search for the golden age and the interest in the gentle savage that had characterised
the previous decade. The hard condition of the
life the savage leads 'binds all his faculties,' and
this is true of Esquimau and Patagonian alike.
And then a sudden reference to the South Seas:

Even the favoured isles
So lately found, although the constant sun
Cheer all their seasons with a grateful smile,
Can boast but little virtue.

Therefore he can but pity them, but more than
all the rest he pities Omai:

[16] *The Task*, book 1, ll. 600 ff.

> Thou hast found again
> Thy cocoas and bananas, palms and yams,
> And homestall, thatched with leaves. But
>   hast thou found
> Their former charms? And having seen our
>   state,
> Our palaces, our ladies, and our pomp
> Of equipage, our gardens and our sports,
> And heard our music, are thy simple friends,
> Thy simple fare, and all thy plain delights
> As dear to thee as once?

The poet's fancy shows him the savage climbing
to a mountain-top to scan the ocean for the sight
of an English sail:

> Every speck
> Seen in the dim horizon, turns thee pale
> With conflict of contending hopes and fears.
> But comes at last the dull and dusky eve,
> And sends thee to thy cabin well prepared
> To dream all night of what the day denied.
> Alas! expect it not.

But poor Omai had died long before[17] Cowper
wrote these verses.

Omai had come to England as an ideal savage;
he returned to the South Seas a mere man. The
'noble savage' was the offspring of the rationalism
of the Deist philosophers, who, in their attack
upon the Christian doctrine of the fall of man,

---

[17] It is said that a later navigator to the South Seas, who in-
quired for Omai, learned that he had died about 1780.

had idealised the child of Nature. Man in a state
of nature, the Indian with untutored mind, was,
they held, a noble creature—indeed, the noblest
work of God. Take him untouched by the finger
of civilisation, and you would find in him a potential perfection. Among his endowments there
must be of course an artistic sense which would
put to shame the artificialities of civilisation.
Omai, when brought to this large test, had proved
to be a pleasant person, but not (poor soul) the
ideal man. What the age learned from its em-
pirical test of men in the savage state was pre-
cisely what every age must learn about its fel-
lows in another stage of existence—that they
are, *mutatis mutandis,* very like ourselves, good
and bad, glorious and inglorious, and that the
state of perfection is placed before man for his
inspiration and not as a beautiful dream of what
existed long ago or, perchance, still exists in some
unsuspected isle of the far seas.

IV

THE INSPIRED PEASANT

Here and there a cotter's babe is royal born by right divine.

—Tennyson.

I read somewhere, not long ago, in an ill-tempered review of a volume of modern verse, the arresting assertion that America would have a poetry of its own, when the stockyards should have become lyrical. What our poetry needs to give it life, this critic seemed to feel, was the vigor of simplicity, emancipation from the literary tradition, especially, it appeared, from Tennyson and the Victorians. I shudder a little—doubtless I was meant to shudder—at the lyrical stockyards and the oblation of blood and offal which this critic would have us bring to the Muse. His figure of speech seems to me vigorous but unhappy. Yet I flatter myself that I can grasp his meaning; there is, when you look into it, nothing new in it. The master workman, who is also a poet, singing as he labors, lord not only of his hands but of the lyre as well—this

90

figure has about him a perennial fascination.
Thomas Gray, for example, had meditated upon
him. The poet is born, not made by the schools;
the darling of the Muse may be the rude son of
toil. Accidents of course may keep him silent,
for birth and fortune affect the minstrel as truly
as the warrior, and many a cotter's boy must have
squandered his genius while ploughing his
father's acres; many a Highland Girl must have
poured out her voice to the unresponsive hills
when there was no Wordsworth by to catch its
passing loveliness.

> Perhaps in this neglected spot is laid
>   Some heart once pregnant with celestial
>   fire,
> Hands that the rod of empire might have
>   swayed,
>   Or waked to ecstasy the living lyre.

Some Hampden or some Cromwell, to whom occasion never offered the one opportunity by which
he might have issued into greatness, may be ly-
ing in Stoke Poges churchyard, or even some
mute inglorious Milton, some inhibited genius
whose fire smouldered and burned inward until
the divine spark finally died. But must it always be so? Might not some one fetch us up the
pearl which the dark unfathomed caves of ocean
bear? May not the rustic Milton be sought out,

and wooed out of his silence, till he is no longer inglorious because he is no longer mute? The eighteenth century has often been charged with chilling poets into silence; but, if so, it was from no conscious indifference to poetry, no unwillingness to lend an ear to young aspirants. England awaited the advent of a poet with impatience, and even sought for poetic genius in the most unlikely places. It was surely no fault of hers if any rustic Milton remained mute and inglorious in the eighteenth century.

When Gray wrote his lines about the poet whose lack of education had prevented him from releasing the fiery genius which resided in his breast, some reminiscence may have crossed his mind of the homespun and pathetic figure of Stephen Duck. Throughout the century Duck was the great exemplar of the inglorious Miltons, and the name was, indeed, specially applicable to him, since he attributed much of his ability in writing verse to the study of *Paradise Lost,* the meaning of which he hammered out in the days of his obscurity with the aid of a small English Dictionary. The career of Duck is adequately recorded on the title-page of the edition of his poems as they appeared in 1753:

The Beautiful Works of the Reverend Mr. Stephen Duck, (the WILTSHIRE *Bard), Who was many Years a poor Thresher in a Barn at* CHARLETON *in the County of* WILTS, *at the Wages of four Shillings and Six-pence per Week, 'till taken Notice of by Her late Majesty, Queen* CAROLINE; *who, on Account of his great Genius, gave him an Apartment at* KEW, *near* RICHMOND, *in* SURRY, *and a Salary of Thirty Pounds* PER ANNUM; *after which he studied the learned Languages, took Orders, and is now a dignified Clergyman.* 'Honest Duck,' as he was called by his contemporaries, had a certain facility in rhyming, but he acquired at once all the characteristic vices of poetic style which marked the age. Still, he did have one thing to say, which perhaps no other could have said with equal sincerity. The poet Crabbe remembered him for it when he wrote *The Village* half a century later. Duck, soon after he began to woo the Muse, produced some verses entitled *The Thresher's Labour,* in which he inveighed against the popular notion that manual labour has a joy and dignity all its own. It has not. None of the trappings of pastoral poetry are really found in the country as the peasant knows it:

'Tis all a gloomy, melancholy scene,
Fit only to provoke the Muse's spleen.

If Duck had any trace of genius—which I doubt —he wasted it by attempting to acquire the airs of a courtier and live up to the reputation which Caroline had thrust upon him. At last his mind gave way, and he drowned himself in the Thames.

Walpole said that Duck had not genius enough to supply what he had seemed to promise, and was 'only a wonder at first.'[1] He intimates that his example was pernicious, since, as a result of it, 'twenty artisans and labourers turned poets and starved.' One of these was Mary Collier, the Poetical Washerwoman of Peterfield, who, in 1739, printed a poem entitled *The Woman's Labour*.[2] Mary's poem, with some additions, was reprinted in 1762, with a short preface in which she gave a melancholy sketch of her life. Her instinctive gloom is no doubt explained by the fact that she read Josephus in her youth and Duck in her maturity. The poem called *The Woman's Labour* was addressed to Duck, and was a spirited protest against the thresher's slight estimate of female toil. The following lines, which sum up what she has to say, are based on corresponding lines at the close of Duck's poem:

> While you to Sysiphus [*sic*] yourselves com-
>   pare,
> With Danaus' Daughters we may claim a
>   Share;

[1] To Hannah More, November 13, 1784.
[2] There is a copy of this rare pamphlet in the Yale Library.

For while *he* labours hard against the Hill,
Bottomless Tubs of Water *they* must fill.

Perhaps with some hope of rivaling Duck's
career, poor Mary addressed verses to young
King George; but neither king nor fortune
smiled upon her. At the end of her account of
herself, she says:

'Now I have retired to a Garret (The Poor
Poet's Fate) in Alton, where I am endeavouring
to pass the Relict of my days in Piety, Purity,
Peace, and an Old Maid.'

The fame of Duck the Poetical Thresher was
for a time eclipsed by that of Henry Jones, the
Poetical Bricklayer. He was perhaps the only
one of the inglorious Miltons who achieved, for
a time, a measure of metropolitan popularity.
Jones was an Irishman, of some slight education,
who made verses while he laid bricks. He happened to be employed in Dublin when Chesterfield arrived there as Lord Lieutenant of Ireland. To him the bricklayer addressed a poem,
*On his Excellency the Earl of Chesterfield's Ar-
rival in Ireland,* which, by great good fortune,
came into the peer's hands, and was read by him.
He at once took Jones under his patronage, and
when he left Ireland, after a brief term in office,
advised Jones to follow him to England. The

advice pleased the poet—bricklayer no longer—
and he had thereafter, in England, a seat at
Chesterfield's table whenever he cared to claim it.
Jones revised the old play, *The Earl of Essex*,
and produced what is in fact a new tragedy—
at least it has always ranked as his own.

In a letter to the Baron of Kreuningen, written in the spring of 1753, Chesterfield speaks
with some enthusiasm of Jones as 'un poëte j'ai
[*sic*] déterré à Dublin, qui était maçon et qui ne
savoit pas un seul mot de Grec ou de Latin, mais
à qui Dieu seul avait donné un génie véritable-
ment poëtique. Je crois que la poësie vous plaira.'
The Earl of Essex was produced with success,
was several times revived, and at last found a
place in Bell's *British Theatre*. But success was
too much for poor Jones. The strain of asso-
ciation with gentlemen, who expected him |to
keep up the dignity of a poet, was so great that
he sought relief in lower company. He took to
drink, and wasted his money. He lost the favour
of Chesterfield by borrowing from one of his
flunkeys. He languished in spunging houses,
where many stories were told of his ingenuity in
escaping from the fangs of the bailiffs. On one
occasion he is said to have won the favour of a
bailiff's daughter by an apt poem on her beauty;
whereupon she incontinently, like Lucy in the

Beggar's Opera, set her lover at liberty. At the age of fifty Jones was run over in Saint Martin's Lane, while in a state of drunkenness, and was very dreadfully injured. He died a few days later in the parish workhouse. He left behind him a score of different publications, some of which had passed through many editions, but all of which, except the *Earl of Essex,* were instantly forgotten when the novelty of a bricklayer turning poet had worn itself out.

The misery in which these poets ended, was escaped by James Woodhouse, the Poetical Shoemaker. When a young man, Woodhouse brought himself to attention by an ode addressed to the poet Shenstone, who undertook the now familiar task of introducing another peasant-poet to the world of readers. In the course of this initial contact with fine society, Woodhouse became the humble instrument by which two famous friends were first brought together. Mrs. Thrale tells us that Samuel Johnson was first invited to her house for the purpose of meeting Woodhouse, about whom everybody was talking. It was Woodhouse whom Johnson advised (the advice is repeated in the *Lives of the Poets*) to give his days and nights to Addison. But Johnson did not share the general conviction that Woodhouse was a poet. He described the

public interest as being 'all vanity and childish-
ness': 'They had better,' Johnson told Dr. Maxwell, 'furnish the man with good implements for
his trade than raise subscriptions for his poems.
He may make an excellent shoemaker, but can
never make a good poet.'[3]

I cannot see that Woodhouse's verses are visi-
bly better than those of his predecessors, although his productive period lasted somewhat
longer and his complete works have been reprinted in our own day. His long-winded poems
are full of the same classicism that all these humble minstrels thought it compulsory to assume.
He, too, delights in verse-epistles to the Great.
The 'obsequious Muse' addresses the 'judicious
Shenstone' or classic Lyttelton, or even soars to
the glorious contemplation of Royalty itself.
With all their paraded humility these homespun
singers seldom write of the people and the life
they know, but exhaust themselves in the attempt
to become worthy to associate—though always
deferentially—with the wits and bluestockings of
London. Says Woodhouse in reference to the
life which he would choose, were it in his power
to choose:

[3] Boswell's *Life of Johnson*, Hill's ed., vol. 2, p. 127. The editor of the complete edition of Woodhouse's *Works* (London,
1896), says that Johnson later modified this judgment; but of
this there is no evidence.

Nor should my table smoak with dainty meats,
But clean and wholesome be my cheerful
   treats;
With faithful friends encircled there I'd sit,
To scan with judgment works of taste and
   wit.[4]

But despite such ambitions, Woodhouse had the sense, if not to stick to his last, at any rate to continue at some kind of labour. He advertised to the world, in the preface to his first collection of verses, his devotion to industry: 'He generally sits at his work with a pen and ink by him, and when he has made a couplet, he writes them down on his knee, so that he may not thereby neglect the duties of a good husband and kind father.'[5] Woodhouse was afterwards steward to Mrs. Elizabeth Montagu, who disapproved of certain of his political and religious views. Who would desire the services of a steward with 'views'? Thereafter he supported himself by keeping a little shop, and died at the age of eighty-five, having long since outlived his fame.

But though the bluestockings cared little for the poetical shoemaker, they were confident enough regarding their own great discovery, the Poetical Milk-woman of Bristol.

[4] *The Leasowes, a poem.*
[5] Clearly this was written before Woodhouse had begun to devote his days and nights to Addison.

In 1783 Hannah More discovered that Ann
Yearsley, the milk-woman[6] who called daily at
her house in Bristol for kitchen refuse with which
to feed her pig, was accustomed to employ her
leisure moments in the composition of verses.
She at once took the woman in charge, taught
her spelling and the simplest 'rules' of rhetoric,
and after a lapse of some months felt that her
pupil had made such progress that she might
safely submit her verses to bluestocking judgment. The enthusiasm with which Mrs. Montagu
and her friends received them is significant both
of their eagerness to assist the development of
poetry and of their unfitness for the task. Mrs.
Montagu had made nothing of the poetical shoemaker, but a female Chatterton—from Bristol,
too—made more appeal. She wrote to Miss
More:

'Let me come to the wondrous story of the
milk-woman. Indeed she is one of Nature's
miracles. What force of imagination! What
harmony of numbers! In Pagan times one could
have supposed Apollo had fallen in love with her
rosy cheek, snatched her to the top of Mt. Par-
nassus, given her a glass of his best Helicon to

[6] I have taken my account of Mrs. Yearsley from my *Salon and
English Letters*, from which the Macmillan Company courteously
permit me to quote.

drink, and ordered the nine Muses to attend
her call.'

This hypothesis is unsuitable to a Christian
age, and so Mrs. Montagu suggests that the
Scriptures, the Psalms and the Book of Job in
particular, may have taught the artless numbers
to flow; whereupon she herself indulges in a
flight:

'Avaunt! grammarians; stand away! logicians;
far, far away all heathen ethics and mythology,
geometry and algebra, and make room for the
Bible and Milton when a poet is to be made.
The proud philosopher ends far short of what
has been revealed to the simple in our religion.
Wonder not, therefore, if our humble dame rises
above Pindar, or steps beyond Aeschylus."[7]

Mrs. Montagu joyfully promises her support.

The rest of the Blues were hardly less enthusiastic.   Old Mrs. Delany circulated the milk-
woman's proposals to print; Mrs. Boscawen sent
in a 'handsome list of subscribers'; the Duchess
of Beaufort requested a visit from Mrs. Yearsley; the Duchess of Portland sent a twenty-
pound bank-note. Walpole gave her money and
the works of Hannah More. The Duchess of
Devonshire presented her with an edition of the
English Poets. All social London and half lit-

[7] Roberts's *Memoirs of Hannah More,* vol. 1, p. 363; 1784.

erary London put its name on the list of subscribers.   When, in 1785, the volume appeared,
it was prefaced by a letter from Hannah More
to Mrs. Montagu, telling Mrs. Yearsley's story
and recommending her to the good attentions of
the Queen of the Bluestockings, whose delight
'in protecting real genius' is well known.   Mrs.
Montagu's name was indeed writ large in the
volume.   In the address *To Stella*—Stella being
the milk-woman's name for Hannah More—Mrs.
Montagu is referred to as

That bright fair who decks a Shakespeare's urn
    With deathless glories.

Similar adulation is diffused through some sev-
enty lines of a blank verse poem, *On Mrs. Montagu*.   Mrs. Yearsley, like the other lyrical labourers, was not loth to address the Great in
verse.   Mr. Raikes of Manchester, the founder of
Sunday Schools, the Duchess of Portland, and
the author of *The Castle of Otranto* (deferentially referred to as 'the Honourable H —— e
W —— e') were all commemorated.   Their in-
fluential patronage and sad Lactilla's melancholy
tale made the book an immediate success, so that
it passed into a fourth edition in 1786.

Lactilla might, however, have been happier,
had she been less successful.   There had come to

her, after the publication of her book, the not inconsiderable sum of £350, which Hannah More held in trust for her.   One is not surprised to learn that Miss More was cautious in paying out this money to Mrs. Yearsley, nor that this caution impressed the owner of the money as mere niggardliness.   A sharp quarrel ensued, which was fully aired by both women—by Hannah More in her letters to Mrs. Montagu and by the poetess in her preface to her next volume of verses.   It cost the poor milk-woman all her fine friends and the fine reputation which they had blown up for her.   She sank gradually from view, and when she died in 1806, was probably as obscure as when she was 'discovered' some twenty years before. Had she been of a philosophical temper, she might perhaps have extracted some comfort from the cynical reflection that her fall had been wellnigh as humiliating to her discoverers and patrons as to herself.   Walpole chuckled for months over the collapse of her reputation, asserting that, if wise, she would now put gin in her milk, and kill herself by way of attaining to an immortality like Chatterton's; but the bluestockings were glad to forget the poor creature and the mischief they had done her, and the pathos of her latter state moved them only to passionate descriptions of her ingratitude.

And then, suddenly, near the close of the century, without warning and without the patronage of the great, the gift was bestowed. England had sought for its peasant-poet with the patience of Job. And suddenly the Lord answered Job out of the whirlwind, and the voice of God was that of the ploughman of Ayrshire. In Robert Burns the labourer became not merely vocal but lyrical. He had the divine fire for which Gray had longed and a Satanic pride which kept him from licking the boots of his patrons. The fine friends which the Kilmarnock edition of 1786 made for him in Edinburgh—bluestockings and professors—tried their best to spoil him by making him over into a Thomson or a Beattie. He was expected to be obsequious, to emulate the Irish Jones or the English Woodhouse. But his well-wishers could not harness the whirlwind. Soaring at a single bound above the mute and the inglorious, he took at once and with ease that consummate position in the literature which he has held ever since.

What does the career of Burns show us about the movement we have been studying and its search for a new art and a rejuvenated poetry? For 'the new poetry' all who care for literature must be, in all ages, constantly in search. What the advent of Burns showed in 1786 was that

such an *art nouveau* could come into existence
without any contemptuous spirit of contradiction
or rejection. For one thing, Burns's career
shows us that force or passion or genius—call it
what you will—is not destroyed or even imper-
illed by education. Burns, though not highly,
was respectably well educated. Like many another Scots peasant, he wanted and he got all the
education he could come at. He knew and said
that learning could not make a poet, but never,
so far as I have noticed, is there a hint that such
education is in any way silencing or restraining
him as he sings of his rustic loves and his rustic
hatreds. He never says that he was a better poet
when he was ignorant, or praised others merely
because they were 'untutored,' and therefore genuine.

Moreover, the literary tradition was in no sense
repressive to Burns. His most popular poems
have their sources in the poetry of his immediate
predecessors. 'Burns,' says Dr. Neilson, 'belongs
to the literary history of Britain as a legitimate
descendant of easily-traced ancestors.' The influence of the popular song of Scotland, of Ram-
say, and of Fergusson, has been repeatedly studied and fully stated; but his indebtedness to English literature has been more grudgingly admitted. Yet the plain fact is that his work teems

with references to his English contemporaries and their forerunners. It is not rash to say that his acquaintance with the literature of his century was thorough. He had drunk deep of the poetry of Pope, Young, Robert Blair, Collins, Gray, Shenstone, Thomson, Beattie, and Goldsmith, and the influence of most of them is plainly discernible in his first volume. He was an ardent believer in Ossian, whom he called 'prince of poets.' Two years after the appearance of *The Task* he was reading Cowper with delight.[8] He proclaimed Goldsmith his favourite poet, and drew a line from *The Deserted Village* to serve as the conclusion of the epitaph which he engraved upon his father's tomb. Goldsmith was reigning over the poet's mind when he wrote, in the *Cotter's Saturday Night,* of the

> youthful, loving modest pair
> [Who] in other's arms breathe out the
>   tender tale
> Beneath the milk-white thorn that scents the
>   ev'ning gale.

What language, pray, is this? And whose is this imagery? Is there no hint in it of the style of the

---

8 Those who wish to examine farther into Burns's indebtedness to his predecessors may consult Heinrich Molenaar's *Robert Burns' Beziehungen zur Litteratur,* Erlangen, 1899. Worthless as a general treatment of the subject, lacking even an adequate conception of the problems involved, the book contains, nevertheless, a great deal of valuable evidence.

Deserted Village, and its 'pastoral' background, prominent in which is the 'hawthorn bush for whisp'ring lovers made'? Burns took as a text for the *Cotter's Saturday Night* one of the most famous passages in Gray's *Elegy.* And the lowing herd, in the opening stanzas of the poem itself, the weary plowman plodding his homeward way at evening, the children who run to lisp their sire's return, the blazing hearth, and the busy housewife—whence are all these?

Burns loved the fiction of his century no less warmly than its poetry. With the possible exception of *The Castle of Otranto* and the works of Miss Burney, he had read every novel of the period that can be said to have had any marked influence in the development of fiction. After reading *Zeluco,* he wrote to its author, Dr. Moore,

I have gravely planned a comparative view of you, Fielding, Richardson and Smollet [*sic*] in your different qualities and merits as novel-writers.

He sketches the outlines of this essay a few weeks later. The author of *Zeluco* is compared with Fielding, whom Burns apparently regarded as the supreme novelist of the age. Richardson he held to be distinctly inferior to Fielding in truth to human nature, and his characters, as it were, 'beings from another sphere.' It is remarkable that the sentimental passages did not please him, but the truth is that Burns's taste called for sentimentalism of a more pungent flavour. His favourite sentimentalists were Sterne and Mackenzie. Mackenzie was, he said, the 'first of men'; but he found a richer nature and a better source for imitation in the tears and flirtations of Yorick Sterne. He couples *Tristram Shandy* and the *Man of Feeling* as his 'bosom favourites.' David Sillar, in his reminiscences of the poet, records a truly sentimental scene, in which we detect at once the lackadaisical and self-conscious emotionalism of Yorick rather than the genuine, though feeble, tenderness of Mackenzie:

In one of my visits to Lochlie in time of a sowen supper, he was so intent on reading, I think, *Tristram Shandy,* that, his spoon falling out of his hand, made him exclaim, in a tone scarcely imitable, 'Alas, poor Yorick'!

It was not in Burns to catch Yorick's playful and amused observation of his own extravagances. Burns's passions ran too deep to beget the froth and flummery that fill even the most delightful pages of *Tristram* and the *Sentimental Journey;* but, for all that he had a try at the colloquial manner and the broken-backed humour of Shandyism:

'The clock,' he writes to Archibald Lawrie, 'is just striking, one, two, three, four, —, —,—,—, —, —, —, twelve forenoon; and here I sit, in the attic story, *alias* the garret, with a friend on the right of my standish—a friend whose kindness I shall experience at the close of this line—there— thank you—a friend, my dear Mr. Lawrie, whose kindness often makes me blush. . . . I have so high a veneration, or rather idolatorisation of the cleric character, that even a little *futurum esse vel fuisse Priestling* in his *Penna, pennae, pennae,* &c., throws an awe over my mind in his presence, and shortens my sentences into single ideas.'

It seems odd that more has not been made of Sterne's influence upon Burns, for it is not merely a matter of occasional stylistic imitation. Burns emulated Sterne's philandering, too.[9] Sterne's career gave, as it were, the sanction of the genteel and literary world to a state of divided allegiance into which Burns's wayward emotions had already plunged him, and made his Clarinda seem to him the Scottish counterpart of Sterne's Eliza.

As Burns responded to the fashions and trusted the literary traditions of his day, so he was content with the technique of verse as he learned it from his Scotch and English prede-

[9] He himself compared Jean Lorimer to Eliza Draper.

cessors. He invented no new manner of speech.
He did not feel, as it were, the necessity of dis-
carding the diatonic scale. He did not write
prose and call it verse; he did not even use the
'loose numbers,' which had been so generally expected, though his songs were indeed wildly
sweet. He himself has told us of the labour
which he expended upon a song, until by continual polishing he brought it to that finished state
which his instinct demanded. Like a true artist,
he loved his technique, and, without pursuing it
as an end in itself, yet gladly underwent the dis-
cipline of it all, rejoicing as a strong man to run
his race. 'There is no such thing,' said Swin-
burne, 'as a dumb poet or a handless painter.
The essence of an artist is that he should be articulate.' To adopt for a moment the figure of
speech beloved in the eighteenth century, we may
say that Burns caught the lyre from the hands
of his forerunners. He did not fling it aside, and
fashion an instrument that should be all his own,
but seized and mastered it. Thus was to be ful-
filled the dream which Gray had dreamed of an
inspired peasant who should wake to ecstasy the
living lyre.

I have no desire to leave with you the impression that I consider art to be mere tradition,
without capacity for expansion, or indeed for

new and amazing manifestations. Least of all do I wish to give the impression that Robert Burns walked dutifully in the path marked out by the multitude who had preceded him. But it has seemed to me useful, perhaps even opportune, to reassert the truth that art, in its universal response to human needs, has the power of focussing and carrying on what is best in the past. It may and does gain by reaction; but it is not its normal state to be consciously or for ever in revolt, to be ever repudiating the work of its rude forefathers, or to be constantly scattering what has been gathered in the past.

INDEX

ADDISON, JOSEPH, *Cato*, 3; mentioned, 97, 99*n.*
Aikin, Miss, 56; and see Barbauld.
Alfieri, Vittorio, 42.
America, poetry in, 90.
Arne, Thomas A., 68.
Attuiock, Esquimau, 25, 26, 28.

Banks, Sir Joseph, 14, 79, 80, 84, 85.
Barbauld, Mrs. Anna Letitia, 38, 39, 56.
Baretti, Giuseppe, 78.
Bartolozzi, Francesco, 76.
Baubacis, the, 15.
Beattie, James, 104, 106.
Beaufort, Duchess of, 101
Behn, Aphra, *Oroonoko*, 74.
Beyle, Marie Henri. *See* Stendhal.
Blair, Robert, 106.
Blake, William, 59.
Boscawen, Mrs., 101.
Boswell, James, *Hypochondriack*, 24; and the Esquimaux, 25, 26; visits Corsica, 46-48; *Account of Corsica*, 46, 51; and Paoli, 47, 48, 49-54; his efforts to aid Corsica, 49; in Corsican garb, 49-51, 51 *n.*; mentioned, 1, 2, 12, 38, 42, 56, 57, 77.
British Essays in Favour of the Brave Corsicans, 51, 52.
Bruce, James, 5, 6, 16.
Burnaby, Andrew, *Journal of a Tour to Corsica*, 42, 45, 46; mentioned 36*n.*
Burnet, James, Lord Monboddo. *See* Monboddo.
Burney, Fanny, on Omai, 81,83; mentioned, 47, 107.
Burney, James, 79, 81, 83, 85.
Burns, Robert, 104 *ff.*
Buttafuoco, M., Corsican, 34, 35, 44.
Byron, George Gordon, Lord, *The Island*, 9 *n.*, 10 *n.*; *Manfred*, 68; mentioned, 31.
Byron, John, 5, 6.

Caroline, Queen, 93, 94.
Cartwright, George, brings Esquimaux to London, 25; mentioned, 5, 6.
Caubvick, Esquimau, 25, 27, 29.

113

George III, 4, 26, 54, 59, 78, 94.
Goldsmith, Oliver, on luxury, 2, 3, 4; *The Deserted Village*, 3, 106, 107; *History of the Earth and Animated Nature*, 18 *n.*, 21, 29, 30 and *n.*; mentioned, 1, 21.
Gray, Thomas, character of, and of his poetry, 61 *ff.*; the *Elegy*, 61, 62, 91, 107; the *Progress of Poesy*, 63-65; Essay on Lydgate, 63 *n.*; the Bard, 65, 66, 67, 72, 73, 84; mentioned, 68, 69, 70, 71, 91, 92, 104, 106, 110.

Hawkesworth, Dr. John, *Oroonoko*, 74, 75,
Heroick Epistle, An, from Omiah, etc., 17.
Holland, Lord, 54.

Ireland, Boswell in, 51.

Johnson, Samuel, on luxury, 2, 4; on Omai, 77, 78; mentioned, 1, 19 and *n.*, 24, 43, 57, 97, 98 and *n.*
Jones, Henry, the "Poetical Bricklayer," 95-97; *The Earl of Essex*, 96; mentioned, 104.

Kreuningen, Baron of, 96.

La Condamine, M. de, 7.
Lactilla. See Yearsley, Ann.
Le Blanc, Mlle, the Savage Girl, 6, 7, 8, 14.
Le Vasseur, *Thérèse*, 35.
Liberty, and Poetry, 64, 65.
Lloyd, Robert, 66.
London, Esquimaux in, 25 *ff.*; Omai in, 8, 27, 28, 75 ff.
Longfellow, Henry W., 31.
Lope de Vega, *El Nuevo Mundo*, 73 *n.*
Lorimer, Jean, 109 *n.*
Luxury, the menace of, 1 *ff.*
Lyttelton, George, Baron, 98.

Macaulay, Catharine, advises Paoli concerning government of Corsica, 43, 44.
Mackenzie, Henry, *The Man of Feeling*, 108.
Macpherson, James, author of the Ossianic poems, 71, 72; *Fingal*, 71; *Temora*, 72; mentioned, 86.
Mason, William, *Caractacus*, 66, 70, 71; mentioned, 84.
Maxwell, Dr., 98.
Milton, John, *Paradise Lost*, 91.
Model Nation, necessary elements of, 33.
Monboddo, Lord, and Mlle. Le Blanc, 7, 8; *Origin and Progress of Language*, 10, 11, 12 *n.*, 15, 16 and *n.*; 18, 20, 21; *History of the Wild Girl*, 12 *n.*, the "Scottish Rousseau," 12; his chief claim to remembrance, 13; *Ancient Metaphysics*, 13, 18;